HOW TO START YOUR OWN BUSINESS

A Beginner's Guide to **Entrepreneurship**, **Business Ideas**, *and* **Development**

William O Ivan

How to Start Your Own Business: *A Beginner's Guide to* ***Entrepreneurship***, ***Business Ideas***, *and* ***Development***

© William O Ivan, 2025

©All rights reserved. No part of this book may be reproduced, stored in a retrieval system, or transmitted in any form or by any means, electronic, mechanical, photocopying, recording, or otherwise, without prior written permission of the publisher, except for the use of brief quotations in a review.

Table of Contents

Preface 5
Introduction 8
Identify Your Business Idea 18
Do Market Research 24
Saddle Up a Business Plan 29
Pick Up a Business Name 35
Choosing a Legal Structure 40
Choosing the Right Location for Your Business 46
Funding Your Business 53
Register Your Business 62
Apply for Tax IDs, Licenses & Insurance 67
Setting Up Your Finances 72
Building Your Brand 80
Launch Your Business Website 87
Marketing & Promoting Your Business 92
Scaling Up Your Business 97
Managing Startup Challenges 101
Essence of High Performing Entrepreneurs 106
Why Startups Fail 111
They Had Nothing—So They Started Everything 116
Roadmap to Entrepreneurial Success 124
Epilogue: From the Page to the Path 131

Additional Resources 133

Bonus Chapters 136

    Appendix-1 30-Day Business Launch Checklist 136

    Appendix-2 Business Budgeting Checklist 141

    Appendix-3 Business Compliance Checklist... 144

    Appendix-4 Business Registration Essentials Checklist......................... 145

    Appendix-5 Checklist For Choosing A Name For Your Business 147

    Appendix-6 Sample Template For Funding... 150

Glossary... 155

About the Author... 164

Preface

Sometimes, a passing moment becomes the spark for something far greater.

It was a routine day at Heathrow Airport, London. I was about to catch a British Airways flight when, by sheer chance, I crossed paths with one of my former students—someone I had taught years ago in a course on *Entrepreneurship*. The recognition was instant, and his face lit up with warmth and heartfelt reverence.

"Sir, it's been so many years. I'm now a serial entrepreneur—and I give 100% credit to you."

Those were the first words he spoke, and they stopped me in my tracks.

He reminded me how, during his BBA and MBA days, he had taken a special interest in entrepreneurship. He was not only among the regular & punctual students in the class but also one of the most engaged. He told me that the practical insights I had shared—on how to start, nurture, protect, and sustain a business—had become the very foundation of his entrepreneurial journey. He had taken meticulous notes of those sessions, and to my surprise, he still referred to them regularly even after all these years.

Then came a sincere request that touched me deeply.

"Sir, please write a book on 'How to Start Your Own Business.' There are so many people—some of them my close friends and relatives—who are desperate to start

something of their own. They have the resources, the motivation, even the vision. But they're lost on where or how to begin. Just like I benefited from your classroom teachings, I want them to have access to that same guidance."

He went on to explain that while the market is flooded with business books, none came close to the clarity, structure, and practical orientation he found in the class notes. He felt that many aspiring entrepreneurs were struggling not due to a lack of money or ideas, but because they lacked direction.

Our conversation continued, touching on many of his batchmates and their current life paths. Interestingly, some of the academically top-performing students were still trying to find their way, while he—someone who didn't top the exams—had gone on to build multiple successful enterprises. **What made the difference**, he said, was **not grades, but *focus, ambition, resilience*, and the *right mentorship*.**

Before we parted ways, he looked me in the eye and made me promise:

"Please write that book, Sir—and let me be the first to share it with others who need it most."

That encounter stayed with me. His words echoed in my mind long after the flight had landed. And so, this book is my promise fulfilled—a humble attempt to share the knowledge, experiences, and practical steps that have inspired and guided many students and entrepreneurs over the years.

This book has been crafted with **one clear goal: to be the most practical, relatable, and action-ready guide** for anyone dreaming of starting their own business—especially **if you're starting from scratch**. Whether you've got a brilliant idea and no clue where to begin, or just a stubborn dream and a half-charged laptop, **every chapter is designed to walk you through the journey step by step**. We deliberately kept the **language simple** and the **approach beginner-friendly**—so you don't need an MBA, a rich uncle, or a shelf full of textbooks on finance, marketing, or operations. From validating your idea to choosing the right location, building your team, managing money, and keeping your sanity—**this book is your startup companion**. No jargon, no fluff—just practical strategies, real-world stories, action checklists, and a dash of humor to keep things human. It's not a textbook; it's a toolkit. Start at chapter one, and you won't just be reading—you'll be building.

If you are someone standing at the edge of an idea—wondering where to start, what to do, or how to make it work—this book is for you.

May it serve as a guiding light on your entrepreneurial journey.

Introduction

Why You, Why Now, and Why This Book Matters

Starting a business isn't just about making money—it's about unlocking your potential. It's about **saying *yes* to your ideas, your ambition, and your drive to create something** that didn't exist before. Whether you're a wide-eyed student chasing your first big idea, a 9-to-5 warrior craving freedom, or a small business owner ready to scale, this book is for you. Think of it as **your roadmap, your mentor, and your backstage pass to the real**, raw, and rewarding world of entrepreneurship.

But let's be honest: **the path to building a business isn't always smooth**. It's a rollercoaster—full of exhilarating highs, nerve-wracking drops, and unexpected twists. Yet for those bold enough to ride, it offers a kind of growth, purpose, and freedom that few other journeys can match.

So, what can you **expect from this book**? **Motivation, yes—but also direction**. We go **beyond the "why"** of starting a business to **deliver the "how."** You'll find practical tools, clear strategies, and real-world insights to guide you from idea to income, from planning to profit. Each chapter is crafted to **fuel your journey with clarity, confidence, and courage**.

🎯 Why Start a Business?

Because you *can*. Because you *should*. Because the world needs what only *you* can bring.

Let's break it down:

1. Freedom & Flexibility

Imagine calling the shots—deciding when you work, how you work, and who you work with. Entrepreneurship gives you that freedom. It lets you build a life that fits your values, not someone else's rules.

2. Purpose-Driven Work

Tired of doing tasks that don't light you up? When you start a business, you choose your mission. Whether it's solving a real-world problem or pursuing a passion, entrepreneurship lets you wake up with purpose.

3. Unlimited Income Potential

Unlike a salary cap in a job, your earning power in business is tied to your creativity, effort, and execution. It's risky, sure—but it's also empowering. You decide how high you want to go.

4. Creative Freedom

You get to create, innovate, and iterate. You get to experiment and pivot. It's your business, your vision, your sandbox.

5. A Legacy That Lives On

Businesses aren't just money-making machines—they're impact engines. They can outlive you, employ others, and leave a lasting mark on your community or even the world.

6. Personal Growth Like No Other

Entrepreneurship is the best personal development program you never signed up for. You'll learn to lead, negotiate, sell, manage time, overcome fear, and bounce back from failure. Every challenge is a chance to level up.

✷ But Let's Talk About the Flip Side

No sugarcoating here—this journey tests you.

- **Financial Risk**: You might invest time, energy, and money without seeing returns right away. That's normal.
- **Uncertainty**: Markets shift, plans fail, and there's no crystal ball.
- **Workload Overload**: You'll wear many hats at first—CEO, accountant, marketer, customer service, janitor.
- **Mental Pressure**: Stress and decision fatigue are real. The weight of responsibility can feel heavy.
- **Isolation**: It can get lonely when you're the one making all the big calls without a team to lean on—at least in the beginning.

Still reading? Good. Because here's the truth:

The bigger the challenge, the greater the growth.

If you embrace the messy middle—if you show up consistently, stay curious, and keep learning—you *will* find your rhythm. You *will* make progress. And when you look back, you'll be amazed by how far you've come.

What This Book Will Do for You

This isn't just another "how to" manual—it's your entrepreneurial toolkit. Inside, you'll find:

☑ How to come up with solid business ideas that solve real problems

☑ How to validate your idea before investing big

✅ How to write a business plan that attracts both clarity and capital

✅ How to manage your money smartly and keep your business healthy

✅ Where to find funding—even if your wallet's currently empty

✅ How to build a business that's resilient, scalable, and future-ready

✅ How to set up, launch, and run your business with confidence

And if you're the type who wants structure, we've got you covered with a 30-day launch checklist at the end. No more guessing. You'll know what to do, when to do it, and why it matters.

Who Is This Book For?

Short answer: *everyone with a spark of ambition*. But let's be more specific:

The book *"How to Start Your Own Business"* can serve as a valuable guide for a wide variety of individuals, whether they're dreaming of launching a startup or looking to make a strategic career pivot. Here's a diverse list of potential readers who would benefit from it:

👩‍💼 Aspiring Entrepreneurs

- People with a business idea but no clue where to start
- Side-hustlers ready to go full-time
- Dreamers tired of their 9-to-5 and craving independence

🧑‍🎓 Students & Recent Graduates

- Business or MBA students seeking practical guidance

- Fresh grads who want to skip the job hunt and build their own path
- Tea & Coffee shop owners ready to turn tea/ lemonade stands into LLCs

💼 Professionals in Transition

- Mid-career professionals exploring a second act
- Corporate escapees looking to turn passion into profit
- Freelancers ready to formalize and scale their work

🏠 Stay-at-Home Parents

- Looking to start a home-based business with flexible hours
- Hoping to create income without compromising family time

😎 Retirees

- Seeking meaningful post-retirement work
- Wanting to invest time, savings, or experience into a passion project

🌐 Immigrants & Expats

- Exploring business opportunities in new countries
- Looking to start local ventures without relying on traditional employment

🎨 Creatives & Artists

- Designers, writers, musicians ready to turn talents into income streams
- Hobbyists wanting to monetize crafts, art, or digital skills

🛠 Skilled Tradespeople

- Electricians, plumbers, mechanics starting independent service businesses
- Wanting to transition from worker to business owner

🏢 Small Business Owners & Solopreneurs

- Early-stage entrepreneurs refining their operations
- Founders seeking tips on scaling, branding, or managing cash flow

📦 Online Sellers & Digital Nomads

- Etsy, Amazon, and Shopify sellers who want to grow beyond the side hustle
- Digital nomads aiming to build a location-independent business

🌐 Coaches, Consultants, and Trainers

- Professionals wanting to create a structured business around their services
- Those needing help with marketing, pricing, or client acquisition

This book is not just for the "Shark Tank" hopefuls—it's for anyone who wants to turn their ideas into income, independence, and impact.

Whether you're just starting out or already halfway in, this book meets you where you are—and helps you move forward with clarity and momentum.

🕸 Your Entrepreneurial Mindset: The Real MVP

Before you dive into the practical chapters, here's one thing you need to know:

Skills can be learned. But mindset is what keeps you in the game.

You need:

- **Curiosity** to ask the right questions.
- **Courage** to take the first (and next) step.
- **Grit** to push through obstacles.
- **Adaptability** to pivot when needed.
- **Vision** to stay focused on the big picture.

This book will give you tools and knowledge. But *you* are the engine. Keep showing up. Keep building. The results will follow.

🕸 Why *This* Book? Not the Thousand Others? Here's Why:

1. **No MBA Required, No Jargon Used**

   This book speaks *your* language. It doesn't assume you're a Wall Street whiz or Silicon Valley prodigy. It simplifies complex concepts without dumbing them down.

2. **Practical, Not Just Inspirational**

   Plenty of books pump you up with "You can do it!"—this one tells you *exactly how*. Step-by-step, not vague "just believe in yourself" fluff.

3. **It's Startup Reality, Not Startup Fantasy**

We don't just glamorize entrepreneurship—we show you the sleepless nights, budgeting woes, and coffee-fueled decision-making *and* how to handle it like a pro.

4. **Built for Real People with Real Constraints**

   This isn't written for trust fund babies or tech bros with seed funding. It's for people starting from scratch—whether you've got $100 or just a fierce idea.

5. **Covers the Stuff Most Books Gloss Over**

   We talk cash flow *before* branding. Mental health *before* market trends. And location, hiring, and burnout *before* scaling. The real order of battle.

6. **Humor Meets Hustle**

   Yes, you'll learn—but you'll also laugh. Because starting a business is serious, but your business book doesn't have to be boring.

7. **Customized for Today's Business Climate**

   This isn't your uncle's business guide from 1995. We've included digital tools, remote team tips, and online selling strategies relevant in the 2020s.

8. **You Don't Just Read It—You Use It**

   It's packed with checklists, templates, action steps, and self-assessments. It's not a paperweight; it's a playbook.

9. **Tried-and-Tested Advice, Not Theoretical Nonsense**

   The strategies and insights are based on real entrepreneurs, real life situations, and real stumbles—so you don't have to repeat them.

10. **It's a One-Stop Launch Companion**

Why juggle 10 books on finance, marketing, hiring, and planning when you can get a comprehensive guide that covers it all? This book grows with you—from napkin sketch to launch day and beyond.

11. **Motivational, Without the Guilt Trip**

You'll be encouraged to push forward, but never shamed for not doing "10X hustle" every day. Real growth, real pace, real expectations.

12. **It's Designed for *Action*, Not Shelf Display**

This book doesn't want to look pretty on your bookshelf. It wants coffee stains, scribbles in the margins, and pages dog-eared from use.

TL;DR:

Other books may tell you how others did it. *This* book helps **you** do it.

Final Word Before We Begin

You're not just starting a business. You're about to wrestle chaos, flirt with uncertainty, and high-five your inner genius—all at the same time.

This book isn't here to preach, brag, or blind you with business jargon. It's your real-talk sidekick—packed with practical tools, sneaky shortcuts, and the occasional pep talk disguised as sarcasm.

You'll mess up. That's normal. **But you'll also move forward**, laugh at your own typos, and **build something that makes you proud**. Just **don't skip chapters**—you might accidentally miss the one that saves you from crying into your receipts at 2 a.m.

I'm genuinely excited to walk alongside you on this journey. Because I truly believe this could be the start of something remarkable—a bold shift that moves you closer to the life and business you've always imagined.

Let's dive in. Adventure (and possibly caffeine) awaits. Your future business? It's going to be *legendary-ish*.

1

Identify Your Business Idea

Start With Why, End with Wow……. Turning a spark into a solid business idea

So, you've got that entrepreneurial itch. The one that whispers, "Hey, maybe I *could* do this thing on my own." Maybe it's been growing louder every time you doom-scroll through job boards or pay $7 for your favorite coffee. Whether your motivation is passion, purpose, or escaping your boss's passive-aggressive emails—welcome to the brainstorm zone.

But let's be real: dreaming up a solid business idea isn't just about throwing spaghetti at the wall and seeing what sticks. It's about tuning into what you care about, noticing what the world needs, and building something that matters—to others *and* to you.

Let's break it down.

🎯 Start with *You* (Yes, Really)

Before you build a million-dollar brand or quit your 9-to-5 in a dramatic TikTok, zoom in on the person behind the plan: **you**.

Ask yourself:

- What am I oddly good at?
- What problems do I love solving?

- What's the one thing people *always* come to me for help with?
- What kind of life do I want in 5 years—and will this business support it?

Forget trends. Forget what your cousin's doing with kombucha candles. Your sweet spot lies where your passion meets your skillset and solves a real-world problem. That's the zone where magic (and profit) happens.

⚔ Spot the Problems, Be the Solution

Most genius businesses start with a moment of frustration:

- Velcro? Tired of laces.
- Airbnb? Hotels were too pricey.
- Uber? Couldn't catch a cab.

So think:

- What everyday annoyances could be solved smarter?
- What services or products just… don't hit the mark?
- Is there a niche audience being totally overlooked?

Talk to people. Listen. Ask your friends, family, or even strangers in line at the coffee shop: "What's something you wish someone would just *fix*?"

Boom—instant inspiration.

🔍 Stalk Trends (The Healthy Kind)

If you're not watching how the world's shifting, you're missing clues. Peek into emerging markets and digital shifts. Consider:

- Green tech

- Telehealth
- Remote work tools
- AI-powered services
- Sustainable anything

Also check out lifestyle changes. Are people eating differently? Dressing more casually? Spending more time on hobbies? All of these hint at evolving demand.

Sites like Google Trends, Reddit threads, and even TikTok hashtags can show you what's bubbling up. Ride that wave.

🕵 Play Detective with Competitors

Think of this like scouting your competition—not copying them, but learning the landscape.

- Who's already doing what you're dreaming of?
- What are they *not* doing well?
- Are there gaps in price, quality, delivery, or style?
- How can you offer a better, faster, more fabulous version?

Bonus: reading competitor reviews is gold. Customers will literally tell you what they want and aren't getting.

🧠 Mix in Some Strategy: Brainstorm Like a Pro

Try these creative tools:

- **Mind Mapping**: Start with a central word like "wellness" or "pets," then branch off with related services, problems, or products.

- **SWOT Analysis**: List your Strengths, Weaknesses, Opportunities, and Threats. This keeps things real—and reveals potential goldmines.

- **Idea Dumping**: Write every idea down. Even the weird ones. Especially the weird ones.

Sometimes the "what if" becomes the "why not?"

📊 Make Sure People Actually Want It

Alright, time to shift from *you* to *them*—your future customers.

Ask:

- Who needs this?
- Are they spending money in this category already?
- Could I offer it in a way that's smarter, simpler, or just... cooler?

Do some low-key research:

- Run Instagram polls.
- Post in relevant forums.
- Use Google Forms to collect feedback.
- Ask your group chat for their brutally honest takes.

Also: lightly stalk your competition. Peek at their reviews, follow their social media, and analyze their audience. Are they raving fans? Or annoyed customers waiting for someone better (read: *you*)?

💡 From Ideas to Action: Pick Your Winner

Now that your brain's overflowing with possibilities, let's get focused.

Ask yourself:

- Does this idea align with *me*—my passions, values, and vibe?
- Can I picture doing this in a year without screaming into a pillow?
- Do I have the skills—or can I learn what's needed?
- Will this make me money, or just give me a headache?

Test your top 2-3 ideas with a basic prototype or MVP (Minimum Viable Product). It doesn't have to be fancy—just functional enough to see if people are into it. Sell a few. Get feedback. Pivot if needed.

Remember: action > perfection.

💰 The (Uncool but Crucial) Money Talk

Before you dive in headfirst:

- How much will this cost to start?
- Can you self-fund or will you need a loan/investor?
- How much time can you realistically give without quitting your day job (yet)?
- Is this a side hustle, or do you want to go full-time eventually?

Be honest with yourself. Not all businesses need a ton of cash upfront—but all need *some* level of planning. Dream big, budget smart.

🌱 Is It Scalable?

Some ideas are cute but can't grow. Others can snowball into full-fledged empires.

Ask:

- Can this business evolve over time?
- Is there room to add new products/services later?
- Could I automate or delegate parts of it?
- Is this just for my neighborhood, or can I scale it online?

A business that can grow = freedom down the line.

🚀 Let's Wrap This Up

This whole chapter boils down to one simple truth: the best business ideas are a sweet blend of *what you love, what you're good at, what the world needs,* and *what people are willing to pay for.*

Take your time. Be curious. Be scrappy. Be real with yourself.

Oh—and don't forget to enjoy the ride. Entrepreneurship is messy, magical, chaotic, and wildly rewarding when you find the right fit.

So... got your idea? Good. Now let's turn it into something real.

2

Do Market Research

Market Research Made Simple (But Smarter): How to Find Your People, Size Up the Competition, and Prove Your Idea Isn't Just a Shower Thought.....

Let's cut to the chase: you've got a business idea. Maybe it came to you in the middle of the night, during a boring Zoom call, or while trying to find something that just doesn't exist yet. Either way, before you go all-in, there's one key question you need to answer: **will anyone care?**

That's where market research steps in—not as a boring corporate exercise, but as your personal truth serum. It helps you step outside your head and figure out if there's a real-world appetite for what you're serving. Market research bridges the gap between what *you* think is a great idea and what your *future customers* actually want.

1. Know Thy Customer (Better Than They Know Themselves)

First rule of business club: you can't sell to everyone. You shouldn't try. Your goal is to find your **target market**—the specific group of people who are most likely to love what you offer.

Start with **demographics**:

- Age, gender, income, education, occupation, location—these give you the basics.

Then go deeper with **psychographics**:

- What do they value? Are they budget-conscious or quality-driven? Are they eco-warriors or tech geeks?

And don't skip the **behavioral** stuff:

- How do they shop? What makes them click "buy now"? Do they compare options endlessly or buy impulsively?

Bring this all together with customer **personas**. Think of them like fictional fan-favorites based on real data - "Eco-conscious Emma" or "Budget Dad Brian." These are your guiding stars for product design, branding, and messaging.

2. Stalk Your Competition (Respectfully, Of Course)

If customers are your compass, competitors are your cautionary tales and cheat codes.

There are **direct competitors** (the ones who sell the same stuff you do) and **indirect competitors** (those who solve the same problem in a different way). Knowing both helps you map the entire playing field.

Snoop smart:

- Visit their websites.

- Read reviews - what's working, what's not?

- Check out their social media tone, content, and audience engagement.

- Use tools like **SEMrush**, **SimilarWeb**, or **SpyFu** to dig into their traffic, keywords, and online strategy.

What you're looking for: market gaps, missed opportunities, areas where you can shine by doing things differently (or better).

3. Get the Intel: Primary vs. Secondary Research

Market research comes in two delicious flavors:

Primary research = raw, fresh, straight from the source. Use surveys (try **SurveyMonkey** or **Google Forms**), interviews (hello, **Zoom + Otter.ai**), or focus groups (check out **UserTesting** or **Lookback.io**). This gives you tailored insights on what your potential customers *really* want.

Secondary research = already-cooked data, ready for the taking. Browse industry reports (via **IBISWorld**, **Mintel**, or **Statista**), government databases (**U.S. Census**, **World Bank**), or competitor reviews and public content. This helps you understand the big-picture trends and where your idea fits.

Advanced bonus? Use tools like **Hotjar** or **Crazy Egg** to watch how people interact with websites—yours or your competitors'. It's like digital people-watching.

4. Test Before You Invest

Use your research to pressure-test your idea:

- Is there a real demand for it?
- Can you price it in a way that makes sense (for both you and your customer)?
- Are there adjacent markets or spin-offs that could become future growth areas?

Let's say you're launching a sustainable clothing line for urban millennials. You already know your tribe cares about ethics and quality. But maybe your survey reveals they want more casual wear, not formal. Boom—pivot opportunity! And if your competitor, say, Everlane, is killing it on social media but falling short in size inclusivity, there's your chance to differentiate.

5. Analyze, Adapt, Repeat

Once you've gathered all your data, analyze it. Look for themes, patterns, surprises. Use techniques like:

- **SWOT analysis** (Strengths, Weaknesses, Opportunities, Threats)
- **Customer segmentation** (grouping customers based on behavior, not just age or income)
- **Competitive benchmarking** (how do you stack up against the big players?)

Then, make it actionable. Refine your offering. Shift your messaging. Double down on what makes you different.

And remember: market research isn't a "one and done." Trends shift. Preferences evolve. That eco-conscious millennial might be a parent next year, with totally new priorities. Keep checking in with your audience and adapt accordingly.

6. Pro Tips for the Veteran Hustler

Already got a few businesses under your belt? Here's how to level up:

- Turn your own work pain points into business solutions.
- Use **social listening** tools like **Brandwatch** or **Sprout Social** to hear what your audience is really saying.
- Explore emerging tech (AI, IoT, blockchain) and find ways to apply them in overlooked industries.
- Consider spin-offs from bigger ideas—just like *Young Sheldon* emerged from *The Big Bang Theory*.

Final Word

Market research isn't just a box to check—it's the blueprint that guides your decisions and keeps your business grounded in reality. The goal? Build something people want, need, and are willing to pay for—not just something that sounds good in your head.

So roll up your sleeves, dig into the data, and use it to create a business that not only fits the market—but helps shape it.

Because the truth is, the more you listen to your market, the more likely it is to listen back.

3

Saddle Up a Business Plan

Building the Blueprint – From Wild Idea to Working Business Plan

So, you've wrangled a business idea that lights you up more than your morning coffee—awesome. But before you start printing T-shirts or selling ethically sourced alpaca socks, there's one thing standing between you and chaos: a **business plan**.

Think of your business plan like the blueprint for a dream house—or the GPS that keeps you from accidentally starting a gluten-free bakery in a town full of sourdough addicts. It's not just paperwork; it's your north star, your pitch-perfect script, and your reality check rolled into one sleek document.

Ready to lay the foundation? Let's build this thing layer by layer.

✪ Why a Business Plan Matters (AKA Why You Shouldn't Skip This Step)

Creating a business plan isn't just a "grown-up" checkbox. It's your strategic cheat code. Here's what it helps you do:

- **Catch problems before they become disasters** (Looking at you, supply chain hiccups)

- **Stay laser-focused on your goals** (Shiny object syndrome is real)

- **Impress investors or lenders** (No one gives money to the "vibes only" business model)

- **Track growth like a boss** (Spoiler: you'll want receipts for how far you've come)

Even if you're a one-person show, this plan is your mirror—it reflects what you're building and how you're going to get there without burning out or going broke.

❀ The Anatomy of a Business Plan (Zero Corporate Jargon, Promise)

Let's break it down. A business plan has several key pieces that fit together like a LEGO set—with slightly fewer painful foot injuries.

1. 📝 Executive Summary

Your business in a nutshell. This is the "elevator pitch" for your vision. It should quickly answer:

- Who are you?
- What are you doing?
- Why should anyone care?

This section is the trailer, not the whole movie—just enough to hook someone and make them want to keep reading.

2. 🏢 Company Snapshot

Here's where you spill the details:

- Your business name, structure (LLC? Sole proprietorship?), and location.

- Your mission (what you do), vision (where you're headed), and values (what you stand for).
- What makes you *you* in a sea of startups?

It's like your brand's dating profile—give the facts, but let some personality shine through.

3. 🔍 Market Deep Dive

It's time to channel your inner detective.

- **Industry Check**: How big is the playground you're stepping into? Growing or shrinking?
- **Target Audience**: Who are you serving, what do they need, and where do they hang out (IRL or online)?
- **Competitor Sleuthing**: What are others doing well—and where are they dropping the ball?

Add in a SWOT analysis if you're feeling spicy. It helps you see where you're strong, what needs work, and how to zig while others zag.

4. 🎯 Marketing & Sales Mojo

Now that you know your people, how will you *find* them and convince them to buy?

- Your marketing channels: Will you charm people on TikTok? Drop SEO magic? Partner with influencers?
- Sales tactics: Direct sales, online store, subscription box, pop-up shops?
- Pricing strategy: Are you the budget-friendly hero or the luxury brand with a waitlist?

This section is all about your plan to attract eyeballs—and dollars.

5. Leadership & Operations

Who's steering this ship?

- Your team: Even if it's just you and your dog for now, outline the roles.

- Management structure: Clear roles, cool titles (Chief Coffee Officer, anyone?), and accountability.

- Day-to-day grind: Where does the work happen? What systems keep things running? Will you hire, outsource, or automate?

Bonus: Show off the brains behind the biz. Investors love a solid crew.

6. Products & Services Breakdown

What are you actually offering? Go beyond buzzwords.

- What problem are you solving?

- How is your product/service made?

- Why should customers choose *you* over everyone else?

This is where you drop your **USP** (Unique Selling Proposition)—your brand's secret sauce.

7. The Money Talk: Funding & Finances

Ah, the section that makes or breaks a dream.

- **How much funding do you need**, and **where's it going**? Be real here.

- **What's in it for investors**? Include how they'll benefit, not just how you'll spend their cash.

- **Financial Projections**: Build out 3–5 years of future income, expenses, and cash flow. Think spreadsheets but make them sexy.

Don't forget a break-even analysis. It's basically your business's first big goal: "When will this baby start paying for itself?"

8. 📇 Appendices (A.K.A. Your Receipts)

This is where you drop all the juicy extras:

- Market research charts
- Product photos
- Legal docs
- Founder bios
- Testimonies, surveys, sketches—whatever supports your case

It's like the behind-the-scenes footage of your business story. Only drop it in if it adds value.

🛠 Pro Tips for Writing Like a Pro (Even If You're Not One)

- **Keep it simple**: No need to impress anyone with fancy terms. Be real, be clear.
- **Use visuals**: Charts, mockups, photos—make it easier (and prettier) to read.
- **Review & refresh**: Update your plan as your biz grows or pivots.
- **Get feedback**: A mentor, advisor, or even your brutally honest friend can spot things you might miss.

🚀 Final Thoughts: Your Roadmap to Reality

A business plan isn't a dusty doc you write once and forget. It's a living, breathing map that adapts as you do. Whether you're pitching investors, applying for a loan, or just keeping yourself on track, this document is your entrepreneurial sidekick.

So grab a coffee, block out a few hours, and start laying out your plan. You've got the spark—now build the engine.

And hey, when that plan turns into profits? You'll be glad you didn't skip the boring bits.

4

Pick Up a Business Name

Are you really confident in your business idea? OK, Great—now it's time to choose a name that makes a lasting impression on your future customers. Aim for something that's not only catchy and easy to remember but also flexible enough to grow with your business, whether you expand into new markets, locations, or product lines.

Your business name is the first impression you make on the world—it sets the tone, sparks curiosity, and often determines whether a potential customer will want to learn more. A strong business name captures your brand's essence, distinguishes you from competitors, and lays a foundation for your company's identity.

This chapter will walk you through the creative and strategic process of coming up with a business name that not only stands out but also resonates with your target market.

1. Understand What a Good Name Needs to Do

Before brainstorming, it's important to understand what makes a good business name. A great name should be:

- **Memorable:** Easy to pronounce and recall.
- **Relevant:** Reflective of your product, service, or values.

- **Unique:** Distinct from competitors and easily searchable online.

- **Flexible:** Capable of evolving with your business as it grows.

- **Available:** The name must be legally available as a trademark and as a domain name.

If your business is going to have an online presence (which it should), your name also needs to be "digital friendly"—meaning the .com domain or a relevant alternative should be available.

2. Define Your Brand Identity

Your name should reflect your brand's core identity. To clarify what that means, consider:

- **Your mission and vision**
- **Your target audience**
- **Your industry and niche**
- **Your brand tone** (e.g., professional, playful, edgy, elegant)

For example, a luxury skincare brand might want a name that sounds elegant and sophisticated, while a startup that creates educational games for kids might go with something fun and whimsical.

3. Brainstorm Ideas

Now the fun begins! Get your creative juices flowing with these strategies:

- **Word Association:** Start with words related to your product, service, values, or target audience and build from there.

- **Mind Mapping:** Write a central theme in the middle of a page and branch off with related words and ideas.

- **Mash-Ups:** Combine two or more relevant words (like Groupon = Group + Coupon).

- **Foreign Languages:** Consider meaningful words in Latin, Greek, or other languages (but research cultural context!).

- **Acronyms:** Create a name from initials of a phrase or full business name (e.g., IKEA = Ingvar Kamprad Elmtaryd Agunnaryd).

- **Play on Words or Puns:** These can make your name stand out and be more memorable—but be careful they aren't too confusing or niche.

Let quantity win over quality at this stage. Write down everything that comes to mind without judgment.

4. Narrow Down the List

Once you have a healthy list of possibilities, start filtering. Use these questions to guide your selection:

- Is it easy to pronounce and spell?
- Is it relevant to what I'm offering?
- Does it evoke the right emotion or image?
- Is it free of unintended meanings or offensive interpretations in other languages?
- Is the domain name available?
- Can it be trademarked?

At this stage, it's smart to check for:

- **Domain availability:** Use domain search tools like GoDaddy or Namecheap.
- **Trademark conflicts:** Use your country's trademark database (in the U.S., that's USPTO.gov).
- **Social media handle availability:** You'll want a consistent brand presence across platforms.

5. Test Your Top Choices

Get feedback from potential customers, friends, mentors, or fellow entrepreneurs. Ask:

- What do you think of when you hear this name?
- How would you spell it?
- What kind of business do you think this name represents?

This step is crucial because what sounds good to you might not land the same way with others.

6. Make It Official

Once you've chosen *the one*, move quickly to lock it in. This includes:

- Buying the domain name
- Reserving your name on key social media platforms
- Registering the business name with your local or national business authority
- Filing a trademark if necessary

Final Thoughts

Your business name is more than a label—it's the beginning of your story. It's what people will remember, refer, and recommend.

It doesn't have to be perfect, but it *does* need to represent your brand authentically and help you build a strong foundation.

So, take your time, have fun with the process, and trust your instincts. The right name is out there—you just have to find it.

5

Choosing a Legal Structure

Choosing the Right Business Structure (Without Losing Your Mind) .....The Not-So-Boring, Actually-Helpful Guide for New Entrepreneurs

Starting a business is like jumping into a rollercoaster blindfolded—you're excited, you're terrified, and you have no idea what's coming next. One of the first major decisions you'll face? **Choosing your business structure.** It's not just legal jargon or tax code fluff—it's the foundation of your entire entrepreneurial empire.

Whether you're bootstrapping a solo venture or plotting world domination with a team of co-founders, your choice affects everything: how much tax you'll pay, who's liable if things go sideways, and how you raise money. So let's break down your options, cut through the legal clutter, and help you choose a structure that fits like your favorite hoodie.

1. The Big Five: Know Your Business Structure Types

Sole Proprietorship: The One-(Wo)Man Show

- **What it is:** You are the business. No legal separation.
- **Why it rocks:** Super easy to start. Total control. No paperwork headaches.

- **Why it bites:** You're personally liable for everything. If the business tanks, so could your personal finances.
- **Perfect for:** Freelancers, consultants, and anyone testing an idea solo.

Partnership: Two (or More) Heads Are Better Than One?

- **General Partnership:** Everyone shares the glory—and the liability.
- **Limited Partnership:** One person runs the show; the others invest and chill.
- **Pros:** Shared responsibilities and skills. Easy setup.
- **Cons:** Shared liability. Can lead to drama if things aren't clearly spelled out.
- **Pro tip:** *Get a partnership agreement. Seriously. Even if it's your BFF.*

LLC (Limited Liability Company): The Business Mullet

- **What it is:** A flexible hybrid of a corporation and partnership.
- **Pros:** Liability protection + tax flexibility + simple management.
- **Cons:** State rules vary, and annual fees can apply.
- **Best for:** Startups, small teams, or anyone who wants to protect personal assets without becoming a paperwork zombie.

Corporation: The Big Leagues

- **C-Corp:**

- - **Pros:** Strong liability protection. Easy to raise capital. Perpetual life.
  - **Cons:** Double taxation (corporate + personal dividends). Formalities galore.
- **S-Corp:**
  - **Pros:** Pass-through taxation = no double tax. Some payroll tax perks.
  - **Cons:** Ownership restrictions. More rules than Monopoly night.
- **Perfect for:** Businesses seeking investment or planning major growth.

Cooperative (Co-op): Power to the People

- **What it is:** Owned and operated by its members, who benefit directly.
- **Pros:** Shared profits, democratic control, limited liability.
- **Cons:** Slower decisions, harder to raise capital.
- **Best for:** Community-minded businesses and member-driven orgs.

2. What to Consider Before You Commit

⚖️ Liability: How Much Risk Are You Willing to Take?

Want your personal assets protected? Go for an LLC, corporation, or co-op. Comfortable gambling your house on your business? Then sole proprietorship or general partnership might be your jam (but maybe don't).

💰 Taxes: Will the IRS Be Your Best Friend or Frenemy?

- **Pass-through (LLC, sole prop, partnership, S-Corp):** Income flows to your personal return. Simple but may come with self-employment tax.

- **Double-taxed (C-Corp):** Business pays taxes. Then you pay again on dividends.

- **Pro move:** Chat with an accountant before you make a decision.

🌐 Control: Who's Calling the Shots?

Want to be the solo decision-maker? Sole prop or single-member LLC. Want to share control (and possibly debates)? Partnerships and co-ops. Corporations? Expect a board, shareholders, and more structure.

☑ Growth Plans: Are You Building a Side Hustle or a Unicorn?

Planning to raise big money? Corporations are venture-capital-friendly. LLCs are okay for small investors, but shares and stock options get messy.

📌 Paperwork & Admin: Do You Like Filing Things?

- **Easiest:** Sole proprietorship or general partnership.

- **Middle ground:** LLCs (still need to file but not too intense).

- **Most complex:** Corporations—think bylaws, annual reports, board meetings.

- **Co-ops:** Admin load varies depending on size and industry.

3. Legal Stuff That's Not as Boring as It Sounds

- **Register Your Business Name:** Make it clever, legal, and yours. Check your state and federal databases to avoid brand heartbreak.

- **Get Your Tax ID (EIN):** It's like a Social Security number for your business. Needed for taxes, hiring, and opening bank accounts.

- **Licenses & Permits:** Depending on your industry, you may need local, state, or federal approval to operate.

- **Trademarks & Copyrights:** Protect your logo, slogan, or million-dollar idea before someone else does.

- **Partnership or Operating Agreements:** Even for friends or family—get it in writing.

4. Hiring Help: Interns, Contractors, or Employees?

At some point, you'll need help. Know the difference:

- **Interns:** Cheap, enthusiastic, maybe a bit green.
- **Contractors:** Flexible, specialized, no long-term obligations.
- **Employees:** Loyal, stable, but come with payroll, benefits, and HR headaches.

Tax treatment differs too. Misclassifying can lead to audits and fines, so check before hiring.

5. Business Insurance: Because Stuff Happens

Even if you're running a business from your kitchen table:

- **General Liability:** Covers accidents, lawsuits, etc.
- **Workers' Comp:** Required if you have employees.

- **Property Insurance:** Protects your office, equipment, or inventory.

Insurance = peace of mind when life throws curveballs.

6. Don't Sweat the Forever Decision

Here's the kicker: *You're not stuck forever.* Your business structure can evolve as you grow. You can start as a sole prop and convert to an LLC or corporation later. Just understand the implications (and fees) of making a switch.

Final Thoughts: Structure Is Strategy

Choosing a business structure isn't just a legal formality—it's a strategic move that sets the tone for everything that follows. Think of it like choosing the right vehicle for your journey. Are you cruising solo on a scooter? Building a bus for a team? Or piloting a jet toward IPO-ville?

Whichever road you're on, make the decision based on **where you are now** and **where you want to go.** Do your homework, talk to professionals, and trust your gut (and maybe a good spreadsheet). Because a solid foundation now? That's what empires are built on.

Pro Tip: Your future self will thank you for thinking this through now—ideally while sipping coffee and not mid-crisis with a lawyer on speed dial.

6

Choosing the Right Location for Your Business -The Real Estate Riddle

Let's get one thing out of the way:

When it comes to business success, **location isn't *everything*** — but it's definitely close to the top of the list, somewhere between "solid business model" and "not going bankrupt."

Whether you're setting up a cozy café, a consulting firm, a manufacturing unit, or an online startup with a physical office, choosing the right location can be the difference between *foot traffic and footnotes* in business history.

So how do you choose? Do you go with your gut? Follow the crowds? Ask Google Maps? Flip a coin? (Please don't.)

Let's break it down properly.

✿ Why Location Matters More Than You Think

Your business location influences:

- **Customer access**
- **Brand perception**

- **Operating costs**
- **Talent attraction**
- **Logistics & distribution**
- **Visibility & foot traffic**
- **Regulatory requirements**

Basically, a great location can make your business feel like a magnet. A bad one? Like a refrigerator in the desert.

✂ Factors to Consider When Choosing a Business Location

1. 🚩 Target Market & Customer Demographics

If your customers can't find you—or worse, don't *want* to find you—you're in the wrong place.

Questions to ask:

- Who is your ideal customer?
- Where do they live, work, shop, or hang out?
- Is your location convenient for them?
- Can they afford and desire what you're offering?

A vegan café next to a butcher shop? Bold. A gym above a bakery? *Sadistic.*
Know your audience, and be where they are.

2. 🚗 Accessibility and Foot Traffic

Can customers get to you without needing a hiking permit or a treasure map?

- Are you near public transport?

- Is there parking nearby?
- Is the street well-lit and safe?
- Is your signage visible?

For retail or food businesses, high foot traffic is gold. For offices or B2B firms, ease of access and prestige might matter more than walk-ins.

3. 🏠 Type and Size of Business

- **Retail**: Needs visibility, convenience, and branding potential.
- **Warehouse**: Prioritize space, truck access, and zoning.
- **Office**: Look for internet access, security, and professionalism.
- **Manufacturing**: Think logistics, space, and proximity to suppliers or raw materials.

Different business types = different location priorities. Match your location to your operations.

4. 💰 Costs & Budget

Let's not sugarcoat it: rent can make or break your startup dreams.

Consider:

- Rent or lease costs
- Security deposits
- Renovation or customization expenses
- Utility bills, maintenance, insurance, taxes

Fun fact: That charming storefront with exposed brick might also come with exposed wiring and a plumbing mystery from 1983.

Budget realistically, and don't blow your funds on the address alone.

5. 📁 Proximity to Suppliers & Distribution Channels

If you're dealing with inventory, physical goods, or time-sensitive services, logistics is king.

- Are you close to your suppliers?
- How far are you from customers or shipping hubs?
- Will transport costs eat your margins alive?

Being 5 minutes from a supplier is nice. Being 50 minutes late on every delivery? Not so much.

6. 👥 Availability of Talent

You need good people. Good people don't want a 3-hour commute to a rundown alley behind a bowling alley.

- Are you near talent pools (universities, tech hubs, etc.)?
- Is your location attractive to potential hires?
- Is the area safe and desirable to work in?

If your employees hate your location, they'll start updating their LinkedIn faster than you can say "team lunch."

7. 📜 Zoning Laws, Permits, and Legal Compliance

That charming bungalow might not legally house a welding workshop. Check before you commit.

Do your homework:

- Is your business allowed in that zone?
- Are there noise, signage, or waste disposal restrictions?
- Will you need special licenses or permits?

Ask local authorities. Hire a real estate lawyer if you must. Don't assume. *Assume = trouble.*

8. Condition of the Property

Check the plumbing. Check the electricals. Check the mold situation.

Do a thorough inspection (with a professional) and consider:

- Renovation needs
- Accessibility (ramps, elevators, etc.)
- Safety codes
- Internet and utilities infrastructure

That "fixer-upper with character" might also be a money pit with asbestos.

Techniques for Choosing the Best Location

Choosing a location is part science, part art, and part... detective work. Here's how to do it right:

1. Create a Location Criteria Checklist

List what matters most to your business. For example:

- Max rent: $5,000/month
- Min 500 sq. ft. with restroom
- Near metro station

- High footfall zone
- Ground floor

Use this to eliminate bad options quickly.

📊 2. Conduct Market Research

- Analyze competitors: Where are they? What are they doing right?
- Survey potential customers: Would they come to your location?
- Use tools like Google Maps, real estate sites, and demographic databases.

👀 3. Visit Multiple Locations (More Than Once)

Walk the area at different times: weekday, weekend, day, night. Observe:

- Traffic
- Customer behavior
- Surrounding businesses
- Safety and cleanliness

If you wouldn't hang out there, why should your customers?

💼 4. Work with Local Real Estate Agents or Brokers

They know the local game. A good agent can help you:

- Spot good deals
- Avoid bad leases
- Negotiate terms

- Understand zoning

Just remember—they work on commission. So stay sharp and bring your checklist.

■ 5. Do a Cost-Benefit Analysis

Compare your top 2–3 options by:

- Cost per sq. ft.
- Estimated foot traffic
- Projected revenue potential
- Additional costs (utilities, permits, repairs)

Choose the one that gives you the most value, not just the lowest rent.

🔔 6. Start Small, Then Expand

Don't overcommit. You can always grow into a bigger space later. Especially in your early days, **start lean and flexible.**

🚩 Final Thoughts: Your Business Deserves a Great Home

Your business location isn't just where your business *sits*—it's where it *lives, grows, and connects* with the world. Choose it with intention.

And remember: No location is perfect. But with the right research, mindset, and priorities, you can find a place that fits like a well-tailored suit—or at least a hoodie that doesn't itch.

7

Funding Your Business

Secure Capital for Funding the Business (Without Selling Your Soul)......

Your brilliant business idea is polished, your plan is airtight (or close enough), and now comes the tricky part: getting someone to give you money to make it all happen. This chapter will serve as a witty guide for first-time entrepreneurs trying to secure that ever-elusive capital.

Let's face it—funding is often the *make-or-break* moment in your entrepreneurial journey. Plenty of great ideas have died in the desert of empty bank accounts. But here's the deal: funding isn't just about finding cash—it's about choosing the right kind of cash. Because every dollar comes with strings. Sometimes invisible ones. Sometimes iron chains.

So, let's break down your options, avoid the landmines, and figure out how to get funded *without fumbling your future.*

🔍 Step 1: Know Your Number

Before you go asking for money, **know how much you actually need**. Not "a lot" or "enough to get going." We're talking cold, hard figures.

- **Startup Costs** – Include everything from laptops to legal fees, packaging to permits.

- **Financial Forecasts** – Build out cash flow projections for at least 12–36 months. If you're guessing, guess smart (or get help). Investors can smell vague numbers from a mile away.

💰 Step 2: Explore Your Funding Arsenal

Let's dig into the many flavors of funding available to you—each with its own perks, pitfalls, and personality.

1. Bootstrapping (a.k.a. The DIY Hustle)

This is you funding your dream using your personal savings, credit cards, or revenue from your side hustle.

✅ Full control.

✅ No one owns part of your business but you.

✗ High personal financial risk.

✗ Growth potential limited to your wallet.

This approach is gutsy and admirable—but don't go all-in without a parachute.

2. Friends & Family (Love Money... with Legal Backup)

A classic early-stage play. Your inner circle believes in you (and probably thinks you're a genius).

✅ Flexible terms.

✅ Support from people who care.

✗ Can lead to awkward Thanksgivings if things go south.

Pro tip: Always have a written agreement, even if it's Uncle Joe. Actually—*especially* if it's Uncle Joe.

3. Angel Investors (Your Friendly Neighborhood Rich Person)

Angels are high-net-worth individuals who invest in startups in exchange for equity or convertible debt.

- ✅ Cash + mentorship + valuable networks.
- ✅ Less red tape than venture capital.
- ❌ Equity dilution and potential creative clashes down the line.

Make sure you're aligned on vision and values—or that angel might turn into a micromanaging demon.

4. Venture Capital (VCs, Big Money, Big Expectations)

If you're chasing rapid growth and billion-dollar valuations, VCs might be for you.

- ✅ Large capital injections.
- ✅ Access to serious industry players.
- ❌ Intense due diligence, pressure to scale fast, and you'll probably lose a decent chunk of control.

VCs are great, but they don't fund hobbies—they want unicorns.

5. Crowdfunding (The Power of the Crowd)

Kickstarter, Indiegogo, GoFundMe—turn your story into a movement and let the internet fund your dream.

- ✅ Keep your equity (in rewards-based crowdfunding).

✅ Build a loyal customer base early.

❌ Time-consuming, emotionally exhausting, and very public if it flops.

This isn't a "post and pray" game. You'll need slick marketing, a compelling story, and probably a cute dog in your pitch video.

6. Equity Crowdfunding (Tiny Investors, Big Possibilities)

Different from traditional crowdfunding. Here, people buy **a piece of your company** via platforms like SeedInvest or Crowdcube.

✅ Raise significant capital from many investors.

✅ Legal equity without traditional VC hoops.

❌ Dilution, plus a lot of investors to answer to.

Make sure you're ready to manage those expectations—and the emails.

7. Small Business Loans (Old School, Still Cool)

Bank loans, credit unions, or online lenders can provide stable funding—if you qualify.

✅ Maintain full ownership.

✅ Tax benefits on interest.

❌ Tough eligibility requirements. And defaulting? Not fun.

A great option for founders with strong credit and a solid business plan.

8. Grants & Government Programs (Free Money, Not So Free Effort)

These programs exist—especially for businesses in innovation, sustainability, or underrepresented groups.

✓ Non-repayable.

✓ Adds credibility to your business.

✗ Highly competitive and paperwork-heavy.

Winning a grant is like winning a scholarship. Free money, but you've got to earn it.

9. Revenue-Based Financing (Pay as You Grow)

Instead of giving away equity or taking a fixed loan, you repay investors a percentage of your revenue.

✓ No ownership loss.

✓ Scales with your success.

✗ Cost can be higher in the long run.

Ideal if you've got consistent cash flow and want to stay independent.

10. Convertible Notes (Debt Now, Equity Later)

Investors lend money now that converts into equity during your next funding round.

✓ No need to set a valuation today.

✓ Attractive to early-stage investors.

✗ Terms can get complex—lawyers required.

This is a smart hybrid, but don't sign anything you don't understand.

11. ICOs (Initial Coin Offerings… If You're Crypto-Savvy)

If your business is blockchain-based, you can raise funds by selling tokens.

☑ Borderless, decentralized funding.

☑ No equity dilution.

✗ Legal minefields. Regulatory gray areas.

Only go this route if you (and your lawyer) deeply understand the crypto space.

12. Strategic Partnerships

Sometimes, big businesses fund small ones—if you bring something valuable to the table.

☑ Cash, resources, and access to new markets.

☑ Instant credibility.

✗ Requires strong alignment and a solid pitch.

Don't just ask for money—show how you're solving *their* problem too.

13. Family Offices

Wealthy families invest through private offices. If they like you, they're often more patient and flexible than VCs.

- ✓ Deep pockets and long-term thinking.
- ✓ Personal rapport goes a long way.
- ✗ Harder to find and access without warm intros.

If you get in, it could be a game changer.

🎯 Step 3: Build Your Funding Strategy

Smart founders **diversify** their funding—mix and match sources to reduce risk and keep options open.

- **Set Milestones:** Break down how much you need and when.
- **Think Long-Term:** Plan beyond just the first check.
- **Prepare to Pivot:** The right strategy today might need a remix tomorrow.

📊 Step 4: Craft a Killer Business Plan and Pitch Deck

Investors don't invest in ideas—they invest in execution. Your pitch should scream "I know what I'm doing."

Include:

- Market analysis
- Clear value proposition
- Detailed financials
- Revenue model
- Ask amount + how you'll use it
- Milestones

And *practice your pitch*. You never know when you'll meet your future investor—yes, even in line at the coffee shop.

📋 Step 5: Learn to Manage Money Like a CFO

Whether it's your money or someone else's—you better manage it like it's your job. (Spoiler: it is.)

Quick tips:

- Use accounting software (or hire a pro).
- Separate business and personal accounts.
- Budget and track every cent.
- Monitor your cash flow religiously.
- Cut costs creatively (without cutting corners).
- Prepare for taxes—no surprises, please.
- Build an emergency fund.
- Get help—mentors, accountants, advisors.

Investors love when you treat their money better than your own.

🚀 Pro Tips for Next-Level Funding

If your business is past the toddler stage and looking to scale, these advanced moves might be for you:

- **ICO** – If you're crypto-native.
- **Revenue-Based Financing** – Great for steady earners.
- **Convertible Notes** – Ideal pre-valuation.
- **Strategic Partners & Family Offices** – If you bring real value.

These methods aren't for first-day founders. But once you've got traction? Game on.

🎯 Final Word: Get the Money, But Keep the Mission

Funding is fuel—but you're still the driver. Whether you raise $5,000 from Grandma or $5 million from a VC, make sure every dollar works *for you*, not against you.

And remember: getting money is one challenge. *Keeping it, growing it, and using it wisely*? That's where the real magic happens.

Now go out there and make your dream too big to ignore.

8

Register Your Business

Make It Official – Register Your Business Like a Boss (No More Operating in Stealth Mode)

So your idea is solid, your logo is poppin', and your business plan is sharper than a new suit. What's next? You've got to **make it official**—as in, register your business and bring it out of the shadows.

Wherever you are in the world, one universal truth holds: if your business isn't registered, it's not real in the eyes of the law, banks, investors, or even your future customers.

🌐 Why Registering Matters (Regardless of Where You Are)

Registering your business isn't just about ticking a bureaucratic box—it's about:

- ✅ **Legitimacy** – You're officially recognized by the government

- ✅ **Liability Protection** – Your personal assets stay safe (depending on the structure)

- ✅ **Brand Protection** – You can trademark your name and ideas

- ✅ **Tax Benefits** – You gain access to business-specific deductions and credits

- ✅ **Access to Funding** – Banks and investors trust legally registered entities

Now, let's break it down by region.

United States

Where to start:

1. **Choose a business structure**: Sole Proprietorship, Partnership, LLC, Corporation

2. **Name your business** and check availability

3. **Register your name** with your state (and file a DBA if needed)

4. Apply for an **EIN (Employer Identification Number)** via the IRS website

5. **State registration**: Varies based on your structure and state

6. Get any required **licenses/permits**

7. Register for **state and local taxes**

🔍 **Pro tip**: Visit your **Secretary of State** website for state-specific steps.

United Kingdom

Steps to go legit:

1. Choose your structure: Sole Trader, Partnership, Limited Company

2. Register your business with **HMRC** (for tax purposes)

3. If you're a limited company, register with **Companies House**

4. Register for **VAT** (if turnover exceeds threshold)

5. Get relevant **licenses or certifications** based on your sector

🔍 **Tool**: Use the UK Government Business Registration Portal for a step-by-step guide.

European Union

Since requirements vary across EU member states, the general steps are:

1. Register your business with the **local chamber of commerce or government portal**

2. Obtain a **VAT ID** (mandatory for cross-border sales in the EU)

3. Apply for **sector-specific licenses or certificates**

4. Comply with **local tax, labor, and accounting laws**

🔍 **Tip**: Check out the **EU's "Your Europe" portal** for country-specific requirements.

India

India's startup ecosystem is thriving, and registration is your first real step. Here's how to do it:

1. Choose your business structure: Sole Proprietorship, Partnership, LLP, Private Limited Company

2. Apply for **Digital Signature Certificate (DSC) & Director Identification Number (DIN)** (for LLPs and Pvt. Ltd.)

3. Reserve your business name via the **MCA portal** (Ministry of Corporate Affairs)

4. Register your business with **MCA**

5. Apply for a **PAN & TAN** for your company (for tax purposes)

6. Register under the **Goods and Services Tax (GST)** if turnover exceeds threshold

7. Depending on your industry, obtain specific **licenses (FSSAI, Shop & Establishment, Import Export Code, etc.)**

🔍 **Pro tip**: Use India's MCA portal and Startup India for fast-tracked startup services.

China

Setting up a business in China is detail-heavy—but doable with the right guidance.

1. Choose your structure: WFOE (Wholly Foreign-Owned Enterprise), Joint Venture, or Representative Office

2. Reserve your company name with the **Administration for Market Regulation (AMR)**

3. Prepare incorporation documents and apply for a **Business License**

4. Register with the **Public Security Bureau (PSB)** for company seals

5. Open a **bank account** in China

6. Register with the **Tax Bureau** and obtain a **Taxpayer Identification Number**

7. Depending on business type, register for **import/export licenses, social insurance, and statistical reporting**

🔍 **Pro tip**: Local legal or business consultants are essential in navigating the multi-step process and language barriers.

🌐 Pro Advice for All Countries

- ☑ Check if your desired business name and trademark are available
- ☑ Consult a business lawyer or registration expert
- ☑ Save copies of all legal documents, licenses, and ID numbers
- ☑ Stay updated with compliance and renewal dates

📣 Final Thought: Make It Real

Business registration might seem like the slow part of your entrepreneurial sprint—but it's actually your **starting block**. It gives you the legal identity, credibility, and protection you need to confidently build your empire.

Because when opportunity knocks (or when an investor does), you'll want to say: "Yes, we're official. Let's talk business."

9

Apply for Tax IDs, Licenses & Insurance

Licensing, Insurance & Tax: Your Legal Launchpad

Licenses, IDs & Other Necessary Evils (aka Adulting for Your Business) ....

The not-so-glamorous stuff you still 100% need to do to stay legal, safe, and stress-free.

So, you've registered your business—pop the sparkling water (or champagne, we don't judge). You're legit! But before you ride off into the sunset with your big idea, there's some serious grown-uping left to do. Welcome to the wonderfully bureaucratic—but totally necessary—world of **tax IDs, licenses, and insurance**.

Think of this chapter as your business's "armor fitting session." It's not the most exciting part of the entrepreneurial journey, but it's absolutely essential if you want to survive dragons like lawsuits, audits, and surprise inspections.

📇 Step 1: Get Your Tax ID (a.k.a. The EIN You'll Love to Hate)

The IRS wants to know you exist (because of course they do). So, you'll need an **Employer Identification Number (EIN)**—basically your business's social security number.

You need an EIN to:

- Pay federal and state taxes
- Open a business bank account
- Hire employees
- Apply for licenses and permits

🎉 **The good news?** It's free and you can do it online in less than 15 minutes using the IRS EIN Assistant.

💡 **Heads up:** Some states also require a **state tax ID**, depending on your business activities and location. Check your state's website to stay compliant—because nothing kills the vibe like penalties.

💼 Step 2: Get Legal—Licenses & Permits Edition

Just because you *can* run a candle business from your garage doesn't mean you *should* skip the paperwork.

Your business may need:

- **Federal licenses:** If you're dealing with alcohol, firearms, broadcasting, aviation, or other regulated industries.
- **State licenses:** Think sales tax permits, professional licenses (hello, hairstylists and CPAs), and contractor licenses.
- **Local permits:** This might include health permits, fire department clearance, zoning permits, or even a simple home business license.

💡 Pro Tip: Visit SBA's License Lookup Tool to figure out what you need based on your business type and location.

💰 Step 3: Don't Let Taxes Ambush You Later

Here's a not-so-fun fact: **Different taxes can sneak up on you like ninjas if you're not paying attention.**

You may be liable for:

- **Sales tax** – If you sell goods/services in certain states or online.
- **Excise tax** – For things like fuel, tobacco, alcohol, etc.
- **State/local taxes** – Think business privilege taxes, city-specific fees, etc.
- **International taxes** – Running an e-commerce site globally? VAT, GST, customs duties are your new pen pals.

@ **Sabrina Papini**, eCommerce tax expert at Avalara, reminds us: "Automated tools, staying informed, and getting professional advice are game-changers when it comes to compliance." Translation? Don't DIY unless you're fluent in Tax-ese.

🛡 Step 4: Insurance—Because Bad Things Happen to Good Businesses

You lock your doors at night, right? Insurance is like that—but for your business.

Here's what you might need:

🌀 General Liability Insurance

Covers third-party bodily injury, property damage, and legal fees. Translation: If someone slips on your showroom floor, you won't cry over the legal bills.

💻 Professional Liability (Errors & Omissions)

Perfect for consultants, coaches, and service providers. Protects you if someone claims you messed up—even if you didn't.

🏠 Property Insurance

For fires, floods, theft, and other acts of chaos. Covers your gear, furniture, inventory, etc.

👷 Workers' Comp

Required in most states if you have employees. Covers medical bills and lost wages due to workplace injuries.

🦴 Product Liability

If something you sell causes harm, this keeps your wallet from weeping.

💥 Business Interruption Insurance

If your business shuts down due to a disaster, this keeps the income flowing (somewhat).

⚖️ Employment Practices Liability Insurance (EPLI)

Protects you from claims of discrimination, wrongful termination, and harassment.

🎯 **Pro tip:** A savvy insurance broker can help you bundle coverage and avoid overpaying. Think of them as your business's risk bodyguard.

🎯 Final Thoughts: Stay Smart, Stay Safe

This part of building a business may not be glamorous—but skipping it is like skydiving without checking your parachute. Protect your dream by doing the boring-but-necessary things now.

Because when the IRS calls or a customer slips on your showroom floor, you want to be the calm, collected CEO who says, "We're good."

Now go forth, brave founder—and may your paperwork always be in order.

10

Setting Up Your Finances

💰 Setting Up and Managing Your Finances: The Blueprint for Business Success

In the world of entrepreneurship, financial management is more than just number crunching—it's your secret weapon. From your first business deposit to managing cash flow, every financial decision you make shapes the future of your business. Setting up and managing your finances properly isn't a one-time task—it's the bedrock on which you'll build your legacy. This chapter will guide you through the essentials of setting up your finances, keeping cash flowing, and ensuring long-term financial health for your business. 🛠️

1. Start Strong: Open a Business Bank Account 🏦

The first step in creating a solid financial foundation is separating your personal and business finances. By opening a dedicated business account, you set yourself up for smooth sailing in tax season, financial planning, and building credibility with clients.

Why it's crucial:

- 🔐 **Legal Protection**: Keep your personal assets safe by separating business and personal finances.

- 🗎 **Tax Simplicity**: Having a dedicated account simplifies tax filing and avoids confusion.

- ❇ **Professionalism**: Clients trust a business account over your personal Venmo or PayPal.

- 📊 **Financial Organization**: Track your income and expenses with ease, making forecasting a breeze.

- 🗃 **Access to Credit**: Build your business's financial profile for future loans and credit.

What you'll need:

- Business registration documents
- EIN (Employer Identification Number) or SSN
- Proof of business address
- A government-issued ID

Pro Tip: Always use your business account solely for business expenses—keep it clean and compliant. 🖌

2. Get Your Accounting System in Place 📊

Think of your accounting system as the heart of your financial operations. Whether you're running a side hustle or a growing empire, a reliable accounting system will help you avoid tax nightmares, spot opportunities, and avoid cash flow problems.

🔑 Accounting Basics to Know:

- 💎 **Assets** = What you own
- 🗃 **Liabilities** = What you owe
- ☑ **Revenue** = Your total income

- 💰 **Profit** = What's left after you subtract expenses

Accounting Methods:

- **Cash Basis**: Record income and expenses when cash is received or paid. Simple and ideal for small businesses.

- **Accrual Basis**: Record when income is earned and expenses are incurred. Best for growing businesses or those with inventory.

3. Tech-Forward: Choose the Right Accounting Software 💻

If spreadsheets aren't your thing (and they don't have to be), there are tools to help streamline your financial management. From tracking expenses to managing payroll, the right software can save you hours.

Best Picks:

- 📚 **QuickBooks**: Widely trusted, with tools for taxes, payroll, and expense tracking.

- ☁ **Xero**: Cloud-based and great for inventory-heavy businesses.

- ☑ **Wave**: Free, simple, and perfect for solopreneurs.

- ✏ **FreshBooks**: Ideal for service-based businesses.

- 📱 **Wix + Integrations**: Manage finances, inventory, and invoicing directly from your website.

4. Create Your Chart of Accounts 📁

A chart of accounts is your financial filing cabinet—it categorizes all your income, expenses, and assets into logical groups for easy tracking.

Categories to Include:

- **Assets**: Cash, equipment, inventory
- **Liabilities**: Loans, credit card debt, taxes owed
- **Revenue**: Sales, services
- **Expenses**: Rent, utilities, payroll, marketing

Pro Tip: Stay organized and update your chart regularly for easy reference and clear financial insights.

5. Master Cash Flow: Keep the Lifeblood Flowing

Cash flow isn't just about having money coming in; it's about making sure it doesn't run out. Whether you're facing a busy season or a slow month, managing cash flow ensures you can always meet your financial obligations.

Managing Inflows:

- Customer payments
- Loans or funding
- Asset sales

Managing Outflows:

- Rent and salaries
- Loan repayments
- Equipment purchases
- Taxes

How to keep cash flowing:

1. **Forecasting**: Predict when money will come in and go out. Anticipate cash shortages before they happen.

2. **Speed Up Receivables**: Offer early payment discounts and set firm payment terms.

3. **Cut Costs Smartly**: Review overhead regularly and negotiate better deals with suppliers.

4. **Build a Reserve**: Set aside 3–6 months of operating expenses for emergencies.

6. Set Clear Financial Goals & Budget

Every successful business starts with clear financial goals—what do you want to achieve financially? Profitability? Expansion? Once you know your goals, your budget will help guide your decisions and keep you on track.

Building Your Budget:

1. **Estimate Income**: Be realistic based on historical data, trends, and market research.

2. **List Fixed Costs**: Rent, utilities, salaries—predictable monthly expenses.

3. **Estimate Variable Costs**: Marketing, inventory, shipping—expenses that fluctuate.

4. **Allocate for Savings/Taxes**: Always plan for growth and taxes.

5. **Track & Adjust**: Compare actual vs. projected spending and adjust accordingly.

Pro Tip: Keep your goals front and center—ensure that every dollar spent gets you closer to them.

7. Smart Debt Management

Debt isn't bad; it's leverage. But, like any tool, it must be used wisely. Take on debt only when it makes sense for your business's growth—and always have a repayment plan in place.

Smart Debt Tips:

- **Shop Around**: Compare loan options and find the best terms.
- **Use Debt Wisely**: Borrow only for growth opportunities—don't use debt for operational costs.
- **Communicate with Lenders**: If repayment becomes an issue, be transparent and work out new terms.

Pro Tip: Prioritize paying down high-interest debt to reduce strain on your cash flow.

8. Reinvest & Grow

While reinvesting profits back into the business can fuel growth, don't let ambition cloud your judgment. Ensure that every reinvestment aligns with your strategic goals and financial health.

Reinvestment Tips:

- **Be Smart**: Prioritize investments that generate positive returns.
- **Maintain Reserves**: Don't reinvest every penny—make sure you have a safety net.

9. Keep the Pulse on Your Financials: Regular Reviews

You wouldn't ignore a health check-up, so don't ignore your finances. Regular reviews are essential for identifying issues before they become problems.

Key Financial Statements to Review:

- 📊 **Income Statement (P&L)**: See your profitability over time.
- 💼 **Balance Sheet**: Understand what you own versus what you owe.
- 💱 **Cash Flow Statement**: A snapshot of your liquidity.

Regular Check-ups Help You:

- Spot inefficiencies and cut unnecessary costs.
- Adjust your strategies to stay aligned with goals.
- Prepare for tax season without stress.

10. Know When to Call in the Pros 👩‍💼💼👩‍💼💼

Sometimes, the best entrepreneurs are the ones who know when to ask for help. Financial management can be complex, so don't hesitate to bring in the pros when needed.

- 📇 **Bookkeeper**: Handles daily finances and keeps your books in order.
- 👩‍💼⚖️ **Accountant**: Ensures tax compliance and financial strategy.
- 💼 **Financial Advisor**: Provides insights for scaling, investments, or funding.

Pro Tip: Transparency is key. When working with professionals, always be upfront about your financial situation—they'll help you make the best decisions.

💡 Final Thoughts: Your Financial Roadmap to Success 🚀

Setting up and managing your business finances is an ongoing journey—one that evolves as your business grows. By following the steps in this chapter, you'll build a solid financial foundation that will serve as the backbone of your company's growth. Financial success isn't about avoiding risks; it's about managing them strategically and building for the long term.

With these systems in place, you'll have the clarity, control, and confidence to take your business to the next level. Your financial health will not just keep you afloat—it'll propel you forward. 💥

11

Building Your Brand

Building Your Brand – The Soul of Your Business

You've solved the funding puzzle, structured your finances, and now you're ready to step into the spotlight. The next vital move? **Building your brand** — not just a name or a logo, but the living, breathing identity that will define how the world sees and connects with your business.

When people think of smartphones, Apple and Samsung instantly spring to mind. Say "social media" and Facebook or Instagram follow. These companies didn't land top-of-mind by chance — they built enduring brands that connect emotionally, deliver consistently, and show up where their audiences are. That's the power of great branding — and it's completely within your reach.

Why Branding Matters

Your brand is more than a pretty logo. It's the story you tell, the values you embody, and the emotional experience you deliver at every touchpoint. A well-built brand:

- **Creates recognition** in a noisy market
- **Builds trust and loyalty** by consistently delivering on promises

- **Commands premium pricing** through perceived value
- **Drives long-term growth** by forming emotional connections

In short, branding is the soul of your business — your silent ambassador that speaks volumes even when you're not in the room.

Start with Your Brand Story

A compelling **brand story** turns a business into a movement. It expresses who you are, why you started, what you stand for, and where you're going — not as a sales pitch, but as a narrative that resonates.

Why it matters:

- People remember stories far more than facts
- A great story humanizes your business and sets you apart
- It inspires your team and builds customer loyalty

Craft your story by asking:

- What problem are you solving?
- What inspired you to start this journey?
- What values drive your business?
- How do you want customers to feel when they interact with your brand?

Whether it's overcoming a personal challenge or championing a cause, make your brand story authentic, relatable, and consistent across all platforms.

Define Your Brand Identity

Once your story is in place, it's time to build a **visual and verbal identity** that reflects it.

1. Know Your Audience Who are you speaking to? Research your target customers: demographics, preferences, values, and shopping behavior. The better you understand your audience, the sharper your messaging.

2. Visual Identity Design a cohesive look that aligns with your brand personality.

- **Logo**: Simple, memorable, and adaptable
- **Color palette**: Evoke the right emotions (blue = trust, red = excitement)
- **Typography**: Fonts that reflect your tone — playful, elegant, bold, etc.
- **Imagery**: High-quality photos and graphics that support your story

If you're on a budget, use free tools like Canva or hire a freelance designer. Stock images and smartphone photography can work well with some creativity and good lighting.

3. Brand Voice Your tone and language should be just as consistent as your visuals. Whether you're writing a social media post or a customer support email, your voice should sound like "you."

Choose a voice that fits your audience and offering:

- **Professional and polished**
- **Friendly and conversational**
- **Bold and edgy**
- **Empathetic and warm**

Use a **brand style guide** to document your visual and verbal identity. This ensures that everything from product packaging to Instagram captions aligns with your brand DNA.

Build Brand Awareness

Now that you have a defined brand, the next step is **getting it in front of people** — and keeping it there.

Leverage multiple platforms:

- **Website**: Your digital storefront. Make it clear, functional, and brand-aligned.

- **Social-Media**: Engage directly with your audience through content, conversations, and campaigns.

- **Email Marketing**: Deliver tailored updates and offers straight to your audience's inbox.

- **Traditional Media**: If your audience is there, consider print ads, radio spots, or local TV.

- **Events & Pop-ups**: Put your brand in physical spaces to connect with customers IRL.

Consistency is key. Whether online or offline, your visuals, tone, and messaging must match. That's how you earn trust and build familiarity.

Engage meaningfully: Create two-way communication through:

- Polls and surveys

- Comments and replies

- Contests and giveaways

- Personalized emails

This builds emotional engagement — your most powerful brand currency.

Smart Branding on a Budget

You don't need a six-figure marketing budget to build a strong brand. You need creativity, consistency, and a clear message.

Try this:

- **Use social media strategically**: Focus on platforms your audience uses most. Post consistently, use hashtags, collaborate with micro-influencers, and share user-generated content.

- **Lean into content marketing**: Blog posts, videos, infographics, and downloadable guides can position you as an authority and attract organic traffic.

- **Email marketing**: Use tools like Mailchimp or Moosend (many offer free plans) to build campaigns that nurture relationships and drive sales.

- **Collaborate**: Partner with complementary brands or local creators for giveaways, pop-ups, or co-branded content.

- **Utilize free tools**: Platforms like Canva, Hootsuite, Buffer, and Google Analytics can supercharge your branding efforts without spending a dime.

Sales Strategy That Supports Your Brand

Your branding efforts should feed directly into a smart, intentional **sales strategy**.

- **Identify your Unique Selling Proposition (USP)**: What makes you different and better than the competition?

- **Know your customers**: Build buyer personas to understand their needs, pain points, and behavior.

- **Be consultative, not pushy**: Focus on solving problems, not just closing deals.
- **Use CRM tools** to track leads and manage customer relationships.
- **Listen and iterate**: Engage your best customers, gather feedback, and adjust your sales messaging to meet real-world needs.

A compelling brand builds the *why*, but your sales strategy delivers the *how* — and turns attention into action.

Pro Tips for Long-term Success

Once you've mastered the basics, elevate your brand with these high-impact strategies:

- **Craft a Signature Brand Story** - Transform your mission, values, and vision into a signature narrative that threads through every part of your business — not just in what you say, but in how you show up. Let it echo in your packaging, speak through your About page, and come to life in the way your team is trained and represents your brand.
- **Empower Your Brand Champions** - Spot those true believers—loyal customers or team members who genuinely vibe with your brand and want to shout it from the rooftops. Equip them with the right tools, exclusive perks, and meaningful ways to share their love for your brand in their own voice. Let their enthusiasm ripple out into the world, organically building trust and buzz.
- **Prioritize Customer Experience** Every interaction — browsing your site, unboxing your product, chatting with support — should feel intentional and aligned with your brand personality. Invest in systems that personalize the experience and make it seamless.

Final Thoughts

Your brand is not just what you say—it's what you do and how you make people feel. From visuals and messaging to the way you handle a return or respond to a tweet, everything contributes to your brand perception.

Take the time to craft a brand that's true to your values, resonates with your audience, and adapts as you grow. It's not a one-and-done task — it's a living strategy that evolves with your business.

And remember: you don't have to be everywhere or do everything. You just have to show up **authentically**, **consistently**, and **with purpose**.

Let your brand be the bridge between your vision and your customer's trust.

12

Launch Your Business Website

Creating a Professional Business Website: Your Digital Front Door 🏠

When it comes to launching a business in the modern world, a professional website is no longer optional—it's essential. Your website serves as the *digital storefront* for your business, often being the first interaction potential customers, investors, and partners will have with your brand. This is your opportunity to create a lasting impression that showcases your professionalism, vision, and the quality of your products or services.

As Amanda Buhse, owner and chief creative officer of Coal and Canary, wisely says: *"You could be the smallest fish in the sea, but if you have a professional website and branding, people will take you seriously. When I started out, I was making just seven candles in my kitchen, but a strong website made it clear that my dreams were limitless."*

Coal and Canary now produces over 1,000 hand-poured candles daily in their expansive 10,000 square foot warehouse—proof that the right digital foundation can scale with your dreams. ✨

1. Choose a Template to Kickstart Your Website 🎨

Thanks to modern website builders, creating a professional website is easier than ever. With platforms like **Wix**, you can select from a vast array of **industry-specific templates** designed for everything from **finance** 💼 and **fashion** 👗 to **consulting** 👨‍💼💼 and **crafts** 🧶.

- **Step 1:** Pick a template that aligns with your brand's style.
- **Step 2:** Customize it easily to match your unique vision and goals.

Need something even faster? Try **Wix's AI Website Builder** 🤖, which customizes your site automatically based on your input about design preferences and functionality—*in mere minutes.* No coding required!

2. Tailor Your Website with Essential Tools & Features 🔧

Your website is more than just a pretty face—it's the backbone of your business. Adding **powerful tools** is crucial for smooth operation and customer satisfaction.

- **Wix Payments** 💳: Integrate payment processing and accept transactions seamlessly.
- **Wix Bookings** 📅: Allow customers to schedule appointments or make reservations directly on your site.
- **Wix Events & Tickets** 🎟️: Manage events or sell tickets effortlessly.
- **Wix App Market** 🧩: Integrate third-party apps for payroll, inventory management, marketing, and more—all in one place.

Pro Tip: Don't forget to add **contact forms** 📮 or **live chat** 💬 for easy communication with your visitors. These can enhance customer engagement and provide a smoother user experience.

3. Select a Web Host and Domain Name 🌐

You've designed your site—now it's time to make it live! Choose a **reliable web host** that stores your website's files and makes them accessible online. Fortunately, **Wix** offers integrated **hosting solutions** with **robust security** 🔒, including SSL certificates for secure browsing.

Once your hosting is set, it's time to secure a **custom domain name**—your digital address. A unique, branded domain gives your business **credibility** and **trustworthiness**. For example, **wix.com/yourbrand** is functional, but **yourbrand.com** is professional and memorable.

4. Optimize Your Website for SEO ☑

No matter how great your website looks, if it's not optimized for **Search Engines**, customers won't find it. SEO (Search Engine Optimization) is how you ensure your website **ranks** on **Google**, leading to more visibility and potential sales.

Here's your SEO checklist:

- **Technical SEO** 🔧: Ensure fast load times, mobile responsiveness, and fix any broken links. Google loves sites that load quickly and are easy to navigate.

- **On-Page SEO** 📝: Use relevant **keywords** naturally in **page titles**, **meta descriptions**, and headings. Focus on content quality, making sure your keywords match user intent.

- **Mobile Optimization** 📱: With mobile browsing on the rise, a **mobile-friendly design** is **crucial**. Google ranks mobile-optimized websites higher!

- **Local SEO** 📍: If your business caters to a local audience, make sure your **Google My Business** profile is up-to-date. **Customer reviews** 📣 can significantly boost your local ranking.

SEO Tip: Regularly update your website with **quality content**—whether blog posts, product descriptions, or industry news. Content that solves problems or answers questions keeps visitors coming back.

5. Monitor and Enhance User Experience (UX) 🤩

A great website isn't just about being functional; it's about creating an **enjoyable** user experience. From the moment visitors land on your page, they should feel **welcomed** and guided.

To enhance your website's UX:

- **Analytics Tools** 📊: Use tools like **Google Analytics** to track user behavior, identify drop-off points, and spot areas for improvement.

- **Testing** 🔬: Regularly **test** the website's functionality. Ensure forms work, payment systems are smooth, and links lead to the correct pages.

- **Feedback** 💬: Use **surveys** or direct **customer feedback** to learn what your audience enjoys and what could be better.

A smooth user experience directly influences your **SEO rankings** and conversion rates—customers will return to a website that's easy to use and understand.

6. Stay Flexible and Keep Evolving 🔄

In the digital world, **nothing stays static**. Your business and website must evolve together. Regularly review your site's performance and make necessary updates as your business grows.

- **Product Launches** 🚀: Introduce new offerings with updated product pages.

- **Marketing Adjustments** 📣: Shift the focus of your homepage or add seasonal promotions.

- **Customer Feedback** 🎧: Adjust features and design based on the needs and suggestions of your visitors.

Pro Tip: Keep your site **fresh** and **dynamic**. Adding new content, visuals, or features keeps your audience engaged and helps you stay competitive.

Conclusion: Your Website, Your Digital Future 🌐

In today's world, your website isn't just a **digital business card**—it's the **heartbeat of your brand**. From making your first sale to attracting investors, your website plays a crucial role in growing your business and establishing your reputation. With the right tools, SEO optimization, and user-focused design, your website can be a powerful asset that drives success.

Building and maintaining a professional website doesn't have to be daunting. By following these steps and staying flexible, you can create a site that will not only represent your business well but also grow with it—empowering you to reach your goals and beyond. ✨

Ready to go live? Your future customers are waiting to find you online! 🌍

13

Marketing & Promoting Your Business

After launching your business and establishing your website, the next step is marketing your brand to fuel growth and attract customers. A strong marketing strategy is essential for turning your vision into reality, building brand recognition, and boosting sales. As Erin Shea, senior director of North America marketing for VistaPrint, wisely puts it, "Customers are the backbone of any successful small business, and effective marketing is one of the best ways to build and sustain your community."

Whether you're just starting or expanding, here's how you can market and promote your business with clarity, creativity, and consistency. Let's dive into strategies that can truly move the needle for your brand.

1. Identify Your Target Audience

Before embarking on your marketing journey, it's crucial to understand **who you're talking to**. Define your ideal customers—what are their needs, preferences, and pain points? When you know your audience inside and out, you can craft marketing messages that resonate deeply.

- **Tip:** Build **buyer personas**, which are fictional yet detailed representations of your ideal customers. These personas will serve as your marketing roadmap, ensuring you speak directly to your most valuable prospects.

2. Leverage Social-Media for Exposure

In today's world, **social media** is your digital megaphone. Platforms like Instagram, Facebook, Twitter, and LinkedIn give you access to millions of potential customers. The trick is being where your audience hangs out and engaging consistently.

- **Engagement:** Post regularly, interact with followers, and share content that provides value (product updates, behind-the-scenes peeks, or customer success stories).

- **Paid Ads:** Use targeted social media ads to reach specific audiences based on demographics, location, and interests. For Wix users, it's as easy as managing Facebook and Instagram ads directly from your dashboard.

- **Influencer Partnerships:** Partner with influencers whose followers align with your brand. Influencers bring their trust and reach, introducing your products to an audience that already values their recommendations.

3. Content Marketing: Craft Your Story

Content marketing isn't just about filling pages—it's about telling your story in a way that speaks to your audience's needs and interests. Through **blogs**, **videos**, **podcasts**, and even **eBooks**, you can position your brand as an authority while building trust and engaging with your customers.

- **SEO Optimization:** Make sure your content is search-engine friendly. By using targeted keywords, you'll attract organic traffic, helping potential customers discover your business.

- **Educational & Value-driven Content:** Share content that educates, solves problems, or sparks curiosity. Think of your blog as a helpful guide to your audience's challenges.

- **Storytelling:** Your brand has a story—share it! Authentic storytelling creates emotional connections and builds loyalty with your audience.

4. Master Email Marketing ✉

Email marketing isn't dead—it's thriving. With a personalized touch, email allows you to speak directly to your customers, keeping them in the loop about new offerings, promotions, and updates.

- **Build a List:** Incentivize sign-ups by offering a discount, free resource, or exclusive content. The bigger your email list, the broader your reach.

- **Personalization:** Use customer data to create personalized campaigns. Target past buyers with tailored offers or recommend products based on previous purchases.

- **Newsletters:** Stay top of mind by sending regular newsletters. Share business updates, industry news, and exclusive offers to keep your audience engaged and coming back for more.

5. Word of Mouth: Let Your Customers Do the Talking 🔔

One of the most powerful marketing tools is **word of mouth**. When your customers rave about your product, it's a strong testament to your brand's quality and trustworthiness. This organic form of marketing helps build credibility and loyalty—essential elements for long-term growth.

- **Encourage Reviews:** Make it easy for customers to leave positive reviews. Their testimonials can serve as valuable social proof that attracts new customers.

- **Referral Programs:** Create a referral program that rewards existing customers for bringing in new ones. A happy customer can become your most powerful advocate!

6. Networking & Partnerships 🤝

Relationships are the cornerstone of business growth. Collaborate with other businesses, influencers, or organizations that align with your values to expand your reach.

- **Industry Events & Meetups:** Attend trade shows, conferences, or even local meetups to connect with potential customers and partners. These events can also position your brand as an industry leader.

- **Co-Branding & Cross-Promotions:** Partner with complementary brands for joint promotions. Whether it's an event or a shared offer, these partnerships can introduce your business to new audiences.

7. Track & Analyze: Adjust as You Grow 📊

Marketing is an ongoing journey—what works today might need tweaking tomorrow. That's why **tracking performance** is key to refining your strategies and improving your results.

- **Analytics Tools:** Use tools like **Google Analytics** or built-in Wix analytics to track website traffic, conversion rates, and ad performance. This data will help you identify what's working and where there's room for improvement.

- **A/B Testing:** Experiment with A/B testing on your emails, landing pages, or ads. This allows you to determine which version resonates best with your audience and optimize your approach.

Conclusion: Keep Evolving 🚀

Effective marketing is the engine that drives your business forward. By understanding your audience, creating engaging content, embracing the power of social media, and staying consistent, you'll build a marketing strategy that not only attracts customers but keeps them coming back.

Remember, consistency is key. Keep experimenting with different tactics, adjust as needed, and stay committed to delivering value to your audience. Marketing is a marathon, not a sprint, and as your business grows, your strategy should evolve to meet new challenges and opportunities.

Now go out there and make some noise—your business deserves it! 📢

14

Scaling Up Your Business

Scaling a business is akin to upgrading from a bicycle to a high-speed train—it requires careful planning, the right infrastructure, and a clear destination. Whether you're running a small business, a private limited company, or any other type of enterprise, scaling up involves more than just increasing sales; it's about building a sustainable foundation that supports growth without compromising quality or customer satisfaction.

🚀 Understanding Scaling vs. Growth

Before diving into the "how," it's essential to distinguish between growth and scaling:

- **Growth**: Increasing revenue by adding more resources—more employees, more inventory, more capital.
- **Scaling**: Increasing revenue without a corresponding increase in resources, often by improving efficiency and leveraging technology.

Scaling is about working smarter, not harder.

🛠 Systematic Method to Scale Up

Scaling is a strategic process that involves several key steps:

1. Strengthen Your Core Team

A capable and adaptable team is crucial for scaling. As your business grows, ensure that your team possesses the necessary skills and aligns with your company's vision. Invest in training and development to help them grow alongside the business.

2. Streamline Operations and Processes

Efficiency is the backbone of scalability. Identify bottlenecks and inefficiencies in your current operations. Implement standardized processes and leverage technology to automate repetitive tasks. This will free up resources and enable you to handle increased demand.

3. Expand Your Customer Base

Scaling requires growing your customer base. Focus on both customer acquisition and retention strategies. Use targeted marketing, social media outreach, and referral programs to attract new customers, while offering excellent customer service to keep current clients coming back.

4. Enhance Financial Management

Proper financial planning is crucial to sustain the scaling process. Carefully manage cash flow, explore funding options, and maintain financial discipline. This will ensure that you have the necessary resources to support growth.

5. Leverage Technology

Invest in technology solutions that can enhance productivity and scalability. Whether it's upgrading your website, implementing customer relationship management (CRM) systems, or adopting enterprise resource planning (ERP) software, technology can streamline operations and support growth.

6. Build Strategic Partnerships

Forming alliances with other businesses can open up new markets, customers, and resources. Whether it's through joint ventures, collaborations, or partnerships, these relationships can accelerate your growth by providing mutual value and expanding your reach.

⚠ Key Considerations While Scaling

Scaling is a complex process that requires careful consideration of various factors:

- **Quality Control**: As your business grows, maintaining the quality of your products or services becomes more challenging. Implement quality management systems and conduct regular audits to ensure consistency.

- **Customer Experience**: Prioritize customer satisfaction and continuously improve the customer experience. Listen to feedback, address needs promptly, and adapt offerings accordingly.

- **Financial Discipline**: Avoid the temptation to overspend during the scaling process. Maintain a lean approach and ensure that expenditures align with revenue growth.

- **Adaptability**: The business landscape is constantly changing. Stay agile and be prepared to pivot your strategy in response to market shifts or new opportunities.

Gradual Scaling: A Step-by-Step Approach

Scaling doesn't happen overnight. It's a gradual process that involves:

1. **Assessing Readiness**: Evaluate whether your current operations, team, and resources can handle increased demand.

2. **Setting Clear Goals**: Define what success looks like at each stage of scaling, including revenue targets, market expansion, and operational efficiency.

3. **Implementing Changes**: Make necessary adjustments to your operations, technology, and team to support growth.

4. **Monitoring Progress**: Regularly review performance metrics to ensure that scaling efforts are on track and make adjustments as needed.

5. **Sustaining Growth**: Once you've achieved initial scaling, focus on maintaining momentum through continuous improvement and innovation.

✪ Final Thoughts

Scaling your business is a journey that requires strategic planning, resource allocation, and continuous adaptation. By strengthening your team, streamlining operations, expanding your customer base, enhancing financial management, leveraging technology, and building strategic partnerships, you can set your business on a path to sustainable growth.

Remember, scaling is not just about increasing size; it's about building a robust foundation that supports long-term success. Approach scaling with careful planning and a commitment to excellence, and your business will be well-positioned to thrive in an increasingly competitive marketplace.

15

Managing Startup Challenges

Turning Obstacles into Opportunities

🔍 Introduction

Every startup, no matter how promising, will face challenges—often daily. Some challenges are predictable, while others appear out of nowhere. Your ability to **anticipate, recognize, and respond** to these obstacles determines whether your startup survives, thrives, or fails.

In this chapter, we'll dive into some of the **common hurdles startups face**, explore **strategies to manage them**, and understand how to develop a **resilient mindset** that keeps your business moving forward.

⚠ Common Startup Challenges

1. Lack of Product-Market Fit

Your product may not solve a real problem or may not solve it well enough. This is one of the most common reasons startups fail.

How to manage:

- Talk to real customers early and often.
- Validate your idea before building fully.

- Iterate based on feedback, not assumptions.

2. Cash Flow Issues

Running out of money is a major threat. Startups often underestimate expenses or overestimate revenue.

How to manage:

- Track every rupee/dollar.
- Keep a cash reserve for emergencies.
- Delay scaling until you're financially stable.
- Avoid unnecessary fixed costs early on.

3. Hiring the Wrong People

The early team can make or break your startup. A bad hire costs time, money, and morale.

How to manage:

- Hire slowly, fire quickly.
- Look for passion and alignment over just credentials.
- Clearly define roles and expectations.
- Build a culture of ownership from Day 1.

4. Founder Conflicts

Co-founder disagreements over vision, equity, or responsibilities can cripple the business.

How to manage:

- Align values and goals from the start.
- Have honest conversations regularly.

- Document roles, equity splits, and conflict resolution processes.
- Create a strong founders' agreement.

5. Poor Marketing & Customer Acquisition

Many great products fail due to weak go-to-market strategies or an unclear value proposition.

How to manage:

- Know your audience intimately.
- Focus on one or two marketing channels that work.
- Build a strong brand and content strategy early.
- Track marketing ROI continuously.

6. Overdependence on Investors

Chasing funding too early can lead to dilution, distraction, and misalignment.

How to manage:

- Bootstrap as far as possible.
- Raise funds only when there's a clear use case.
- Choose investors who align with your vision, not just your valuation.

7. Burnout and Mental Stress

Founders often carry heavy workloads and emotional pressure, risking burnout.

How to manage:

- Prioritize mental and physical health.

- Build a support system (mentors, co-founders, family).
- Delegate and don't try to do everything yourself.
- Take breaks and unplug intentionally.

8. Inability to Adapt

Markets change, customer behavior shifts, and new competitors emerge. Startups that can't pivot die out.

How to manage:

- Stay close to customer feedback.
- Build flexibility into your business model.
- Be willing to let go of your initial idea if data tells you so.

🔑 Strategic Tips for Overcoming Challenges

1. Break Problems into Smaller Parts

Don't get overwhelmed. Tackle one issue at a time with clear next steps.

2. Maintain a Learning Mindset

Every challenge is a chance to learn. Treat problems as data, not disasters.

3. Build a Feedback Loop

Surround yourself with advisors, mentors, and a team that can challenge your thinking constructively.

4. Embrace Transparency

Be honest with your team during tough times. It builds trust and resilience.

5. Track Metrics That Matter

Use KPIs to monitor the health of your business: cash runway, customer acquisition cost, churn rate, etc.

✳ Long-Term Resilience: Developing a Founder's Mindset

- **Be flexible with the path, but stubborn about the vision.**
- **Accept uncertainty as normal.**
- **Celebrate small wins.**
- **Don't compare your Chapter 1 to someone else's Chapter 10.**

📝 Summary

Startup challenges are not signs of failure—they are the *curriculum* of entrepreneurship. Every obstacle is an opportunity to refine your product, strengthen your team, and sharpen your strategy.

If you prepare for challenges instead of fearing them, and build a mindset of **adaptability and grit**, you'll dramatically improve your chances of not just surviving—but succeeding.

16

Essence of High Performing Entrepreneurs

🔑 *Blueprint of a Modern-Day Entrepreneur: Traits, Rituals & Mindsets That Forge Success*

Entrepreneurship isn't a title—it's a way of thinking, acting, and growing. The world's most successful founders don't rely on luck. They design their days, evolve with intention, and embody principles that compound over time. Here's a distilled, re-engineered version of what truly sets them apart.

🧬 Core Entrepreneurial DNA: Who They Are

1. **Purpose-Driven, Not Profit-Obsessed** Money follows meaning. The best entrepreneurs are fueled by purpose and see revenue as a byproduct of delivering impact.

2. **Vision Carvers** They don't just think big—they see clearly. Their vision is sharp enough to guide others and flexible enough to evolve.

3. **Adaptive Strategists** Change doesn't scare them—it excites them. They adjust their sails with grace, speed, and intention.

4. **Courageous Risk-Takers** They place smart bets—not blind ones. Risk is a calculated partner, not an enemy.

5. **Relentlessly Curious** They ask better questions, stay humble learners, and treat every moment as an opportunity to grow.

6. **Solution Architects** Complaints don't linger. Problems trigger solutions. They seek friction and turn it into value.

7. **Disciplined Dreamers** Big ideas backed by structured execution. Passion alone isn't their weapon—discipline is.

8. **Persistent Builders** Setbacks don't derail them. They see failure not as the end, but as raw material for reinvention.

⌛ High-Performance Habits: How They Operate

🐚 Morning Momentum

- **Intention > Reaction**: No emails, no scrolling. Mornings are sacred. Think reflection, journaling, or silence.

- **Top 3 Focus**: Clarity on the three non-negotiables that must move forward today.

🧠 Mind as a Weapon

- **Time-Travel Thinking**: Beat procrastination by asking: *"What can I do now to help Future Me succeed?"*

- **Notebook Overload**: Everything goes on paper—ideas, learnings, to-dos. Free the mind, focus the brain.

❀ Daily Execution Rituals

- **Calendar-Driven, Not List-Burdened**: Everything scheduled. Nothing floats. Tasks live on the calendar.

- **2-Hour Deep Work Sprints**: Morning blocks reserved for the Most Important Task (MIT).

💡 Learning as Fuel

- 30 minutes daily of reading, podcasting, or studying trends = exponential compound growth in insight.

- They learn fast—and unlearn even faster.

🧘 Health, Energy & Focus

- **Movement Daily**: Even 20 minutes a day—walks, lifting, yoga—sharpens mind and body.

- **Mindfulness Practice**: Meditation or deep breathing to reset, recenter, refocus.

- **Clean Diet & Solid Sleep**: Cognitive clarity starts with biological self-respect.

🌐 Relationship Capital: The Invisible Accelerator

- **Proactive Networking**: At least one outreach per day—email, DM, or thoughtful comment.

- **Stakeholder Listening**: They're accessible, not isolated. Employees, customers, and partners are heard—and seen.

- **Customer First**: Internal (team) and external (clients) voices shape every decision.

📊 Strategic Thinking in Action

■ Metrics-Driven Decisions

- Daily dashboard check: Revenue, leads, churn, conversions.

- No guesses. Only data-informed moves.

Deliver Real Value

- Products don't sell. Transformations do.
- The goal: leave customers *better* than you found them.

Clarity in Communication

- If you can't explain it simply, it's not ready.
- Great ideas mean nothing without articulation.

Laser Focus via Elimination

- Say "no" 10x more than you say "yes."
- Eliminate distractions, avoid busywork, and never people-please at the cost of the mission.

Leadership Traits that Scale Companies

1. **Builder of Specialist Teams** Founders aren't great at everything—but they find people who are. They connect the dots others miss.

2. **Empowering Leaders (Not Bosses)** They don't just delegate—they inspire ownership. Their team isn't managed, it's motivated.

3. **Gratitude-Driven Culture** Daily appreciation. Big or small. They recognize effort and celebrate progress.

4. **Always in Beta** No version is final. Their mindset, their product, their leadership—constantly iterating.

Final Thought: The Entrepreneur's Equation

Clarity + Discipline + Adaptability + Consistent Action = Unstoppable Momentum

There's no one-size blueprint. But there *is* a common thread: **successful entrepreneurs run their days like pilots fly planes—calculated, intentional, and with eyes always on the horizon.**

17

Why Startups Fail: Lessons From the Frontlines of Entrepreneurship

Launching a startup is one of the most exhilarating, yet unforgiving, journeys in business. Entrepreneurs bring fresh ideas, energy, and the ambition to change the world. But harsh statistics cast a long shadow—*half of all startups fail within five years, and only one in three survives beyond a decade.* The silver lining? Failure isn't random. It's the outcome of specific, repeated mistakes that can be studied—and avoided.

This chapter explores the *core reasons startups fail*—drawn from real-world experiences, empirical data, and expert advice—and offers proactive strategies to stay ahead of the pitfalls.

1. Cash Flow Mismanagement: The Startup Killer

Cash is the oxygen of any business. Many startups suffocate because they don't manage it wisely.

Startups often overestimate revenue and underestimate expenses. Whether it's underpricing products, overspending too soon, or ignoring burn rates, these missteps can drain capital fast. Factor in investor pressure, surprise costs, and delayed income, and the runway shortens quickly. If not managed carefully, failure can arrive faster than expected.

Lesson: Maintain laser-sharp visibility on cash flow. Build financial forecasts, monitor burn rate, and plan for worst-case scenarios. Always have a runway, and never rely on future funding as a certainty.

2. Solving the Wrong Problem: Lack of Market Need

You might build a great product—but if no one wants it, it won't matter.

Too many startups create solutions in search of a problem, driven by personal excitement rather than validated customer demand. Misjudging market need is not just a risk—it's one of the top reasons startups fail.

Lesson: Validate your idea with real customers before launching. Conduct surveys, interviews, and A/B tests. Stay obsessed with the *problem*, not just the *solution*.

3. Weak Business Models and Flawed Plans

Ideas are cheap. Execution is everything. But execution without planning is gambling.

Some entrepreneurs skip rigorous planning, hoping hustle alone will fill the gaps. Others create overcomplicated plans that ignore basic realities like pricing, competition, or supply chains.

Lesson: Develop a business model that clearly outlines how you create, deliver, and capture value. Keep your plan lean but realistic—identify revenue streams, customer acquisition cost, and timeline milestones.

4. Poor Leadership and Team Dysfunction

Leadership is more than vision—it's coordination, delegation, and resilience. Startups often suffer from unclear roles, misaligned co-founders, or a lack of emotional intelligence at the top.

As companies grow, founders must evolve from doers to leaders. Those who can't transition, or who micromanage everything, limit their company's potential.

Lesson: Surround yourself with people smarter than you in areas you're weak. Communicate clearly, delegate intentionally, and invest in developing leadership skills early.

5. Ignoring Marketing or Doing It Wrong

A brilliant product without visibility is invisible.

Startups sometimes rely solely on word of mouth or social media without a data-driven marketing strategy. Others burn through budgets on campaigns that aren't aligned with their brand or customers.

Lesson: Define your target market. Create clear positioning. Invest in customer acquisition channels with measurable ROI—SEO, paid ads, partnerships, and especially customer referrals. Your marketing should speak to a real problem your audience experiences.

6. Resistance to Change and Market Adaptation

Markets evolve. Customer preferences shift. Competitors emerge. Startups that fail to adapt—or worse, refuse to—get left behind.

Even successful ideas have an expiry date if not refined or pivoted. Think of Blockbuster, Nokia, or Kodak—giants toppled by stagnation.

Lesson: Stay close to the customer. Stay humble. When the data, market, or feedback suggests a pivot—move fast. Agility is a competitive advantage.

7. Hiring the Wrong People

A startup's first hires are critical. A weak team can derail progress, while a strong one can elevate a rough idea into a success story.

Startups sometimes prioritize cheap labor, over-rely on friends, or neglect culture fit. Others fail to upskill or invest in team development.

Lesson: Hire slowly and wisely. Look beyond resumes—focus on adaptability, attitude, and cultural alignment. Build a team where people take ownership and share the vision.

8. Not Leveraging Technology

In a digital world, doing things manually or using outdated systems is like running a marathon in flip-flops. Startups that ignore automation, data analytics, or digital tools waste precious time and money.

Lesson: Identify areas where technology can streamline your operations—marketing, accounting, sales, customer support. Embrace tools that let you scale smarter, not just harder.

9. Failure to Learn and Accept Feedback

Startups are feedback loops. Every customer complaint, lost deal, or failed experiment holds a lesson. Yet many founders block out critique, clinging emotionally to their ideas.

Lesson: Develop thick skin and an open mind. Seek mentorship, test your assumptions often, and treat failures as tuition for long-term success.

10. Burnout and Founder Overload

Startups are intense. Founders often take on multiple roles—CEO, marketer, designer, customer support. Without boundaries or support, burnout becomes inevitable, draining passion and productivity.

Lesson: Don't be a martyr for your business. Delegate early. Take breaks. Surround yourself with a support system. A healthy founder is a startup's greatest asset.

11. Neglecting Culture and Customer Experience

Startups that grow without an intentional culture often unravel internally. Those that ignore the customer experience lose repeat business and reputation.

Lesson: Build your company from day one with values, mission, and culture in mind. Treat every customer interaction as brand-defining. Small businesses can win on personalization—leverage it.

Final Thoughts: Failure is Feedback

Startup failure is painful—but it's rarely mysterious. The reasons are recurring, identifiable, and—most importantly—preventable. Each failed venture is a blueprint of what not to do. The more entrepreneurs study failure, the better equipped they are to write a different story.

Success doesn't come from avoiding all mistakes. It comes from *recognizing* them early, *learning* from them fast, and *pivoting* with courage and clarity.

If you're starting a business, don't aim for perfection. Aim to *stay aware*, *stay adaptable*, and *stay learning*.

18

They Had Nothing—So They Started Everything

What is Holding You Back

Let me put the record straight: greatness doesn't come with a golden ticket. It doesn't ask for permission, wait for credentials, or check your background. Successful entrepreneurs aren't superheroes. They're not born with secret knowledge, perfect timing, or trust funds. **They weren't backed by flawless horoscopes, overflowing bank accounts, or polished degrees**—yet they dared to step into the chaotic, uncharted world of entrepreneurship, guided only by strong belief and bold intent. Some of the most iconic entrepreneurs of our time didn't have money, connections, or even a clear plan. What they had was strong *belief*. What they had was *boldness*. What they had was the decision to start—right where they were, with what they had. "In fact, most of the world's most celebrated business icons started with **nothing but a fire in their belly and a belief that they could do something more**.

This chapter is about those people—Oprah Winfrey, Mark Zuckerberg, Richard Branson, and many others **who turned doubt into drive** and **limitations into legacy. And if they could start from nothing… so can you.**

❋ OPRAH WINFREY: From Dirt Roads to Global Impact

- **Background:** Raised in poverty, faced abuse, and overcame countless personal traumas.
- **Journey:** Used her voice and empathy to connect with millions, eventually building a media empire.
- **Lesson:** Your past does not determine your potential—it fuels your power to rise.

💡 MARK ZUCKERBERG: The Dorm Room Disruptor

- **Background:** College student with no business background.
- **Journey:** Created a simple platform to connect students—turned it into Facebook.
- **Lesson:** You don't need to know everything—you just need to begin.

🚀 RICHARD BRANSON: The Rebel Entrepreneur

- **Background:** Dropped out of school, struggled with dyslexia, no formal training.
- **Journey:** Launched Virgin from a magazine to an airline and beyond.
- **Lesson:** Inexperience can be your superpower.

🛏 RITESH AGARWAL – FOUNDER OF OYO ROOMS

- **Background:** Small-town boy from Odisha, India. Dropped out of college. No formal training or business network.

- **Journey:** Spotted a gap in India's budget hotel space, launched OYO at 19. Faced skepticism, rejection, and countless hurdles. Today, OYO operates in 80+ countries.
- **Lesson:** You don't need age, degrees, or a family business—you need **vision and relentlessness**.

Jan Koum – Founder of WhatsApp

- **Background:** Grew up in a small village in Ukraine, immigrated to the U.S. with his mother, lived on food stamps, and worked as a janitor.
- **Journey:** Taught himself computer skills, eventually co-founded WhatsApp, which was sold to Facebook for $19 billion.
- **Lesson:** A tough past doesn't define your future—resourcefulness does.

Sophia Amoruso – Founder of Nasty Gal and Girlboss

- **Background:** Dropped out of school, lived off dumpster diving and odd jobs.
- **Journey:** Started by selling vintage clothes on eBay. Grew Nasty Gal into a multi-million-dollar fashion brand.
- **Lesson:** Hustle, taste, and timing can beat experience.

Howard Schultz – CEO of Starbucks

- **Background:** Grew up in a housing project in Brooklyn. First in his family to attend college.
- **Journey:** Joined Starbucks when it was just a local coffee shop. Transformed it into a global brand.
- **Lesson:** Vision and grit can elevate humble beginnings.

🏠 Daymond John – Founder of FUBU & Investor on Shark Tank

- **Background:** Grew up in Queens, raised by a single mother, struggled with dyslexia.
- **Journey:** Started sewing hats and T-shirts at home. Turned FUBU into a $6 billion fashion empire.
- **Lesson:** You don't need capital—you need creativity and grind.

🪨 Jack Ma – Founder of Alibaba

- **Background:** Failed university entrance exams twice, rejected from dozens of jobs—including KFC.
- **Journey:** Taught himself English, later started Alibaba with no tech background. Built one of the largest e-commerce companies in the world.
- **Lesson:** Persistence beats rejection, every time.

🔑 JAN KOUM – FOUNDER OF WHATSAPP

- **Background:** Grew up in a small Ukrainian village, immigrated to the U.S., lived on food stamps, worked as a janitor.
- **Journey:** Taught himself coding, co-founded WhatsApp, sold it to Facebook for $19 billion.
- **Lesson:** A tough past doesn't define your future—**resourcefulness does**.

📱 SOPHIA AMORUSO – FOUNDER OF NASTY GAL & GIRLBOSS

- **Background:** Dropped out of school, lived off odd jobs and dumpster diving.

- **Journey:** Started reselling vintage clothes on eBay. Built a multi-million dollar fashion brand.

- **Lesson: Hustle, taste, and timing** can beat experience.

🎨 HOWARD SCHULTZ – CEO OF STARBUCKS

- **Background:** Raised in a housing project in Brooklyn. First in his family to go to college.

- **Journey:** Took Starbucks from a local coffee shop to a global icon.

- **Lesson: Vision and grit** can elevate the most modest beginnings.

🏠 DAYMOND JOHN – FOUNDER OF FUBU & SHARK TANK INVESTOR

- **Background:** Grew up in Queens, raised by a single mom, battled dyslexia.

- **Journey:** Started sewing T-shirts in his home. Built FUBU into a $6 billion brand.

- **Lesson:** You don't need capital—you need **creativity and grind**.

📱 JACK MA – FOUNDER OF ALIBABA

- **Background:** Failed college entrance exams, rejected by over 30 jobs (even KFC).

- **Journey:** Learned English, embraced the internet early, built Alibaba into an e-commerce titan.

- **Lesson: Persistence beats rejection**, every time.

🔥 THE COMMON THREAD: They Started *Anyway*

They didn't wait until the stars aligned. They didn't wait to feel "ready." They didn't hold out for funding, approval, or permission.

They **just started**—with fear in their pockets and fire in their hearts.

You may not have money, experience, or connections. That's okay. What you *do* have is the ability to take the first step. Right now.

🛠 Principles to Break Free and Begin

1. **Start Small, But Start Bold.**

   A tiny idea can grow into a global force—if you act on it. Don't underestimate your beginning.

2. **Turn Fear into Fuel.**

   Every entrepreneur feels fear. Use it to sharpen your focus, not to paralyze your progress.

3. **Redefine "Qualifications."**

   Real-world hustle, curiosity, and grit often outweigh formal education or experience.

4. **Make Mistakes Fast.**

   You learn faster by doing. Start messy, fail forward, and adjust quickly.

5. **Surround Yourself with Energy.**

   Find people who ignite your vision, not drain it. Community matters more than credentials.

💡 Key Takeaway

- No **age**, **degree**, or **background** is a barrier to starting a business.
- What really matters is your **drive**, **creativity**, **resilience**, and the **willingness to learn**.

✺ You Already Have What It Takes

You don't need more time. You don't need more talent. You just need the *courage to begin*. The belief that your version of success is waiting—not for the perfect plan, but for your imperfect action.

Because just like Oprah, Mark, and Richard—you don't need to have everything.

You just need to *start everything*.

"Try the simple exercise below—it's designed to help you break through mental barriers and unlock fresh momentum."

A Small Exercise to Supercharge Your Mind & Soul

📝 *Your Turn: Break the Barrier*

Take 10 quiet minutes. No distractions. Just you and this page.

Step 1: Write down the top 3 reasons you think you're "not ready" to start your business.

(Be honest—maybe it's age, lack of money, no experience, fear of failure, etc.)

Step 2: Now, for each one, write a counter-belief. Flip the script.

Examples:

- *"I don't have experience"* → *"I will learn faster by doing."*

- "I don't have money" → "Creativity beats capital—I'll start lean."

- "I'm too young/too old" → "Success has no age limit."

Step 3: Write this sentence and fill in the blank:

"Even though I don't have ___, I'm starting anyway—because I believe ___."

✅ Commit to One Tiny Action Today

Big businesses start with small, bold moves. **What's one simple step you can take today?** It could be researching a domain name, sketching a logo, or texting a mentor.

Write it here →

Today, I will: _____

Final Word

The only thing separating you from the entrepreneurs you admire… is **action**.
They didn't wait for perfect. They just started.

So now the question is:

Will you?

19

Roadmap to Entrepreneurial Success

Let me consolidate all the key learnings we've covered in the previous chapters. If you're looking for a practical blueprint to guide you consistently and increase your chances of success in running a startup, this is it — your roadmap to entrepreneurial success.

🎯 Mindset & Philosophy: The Foundation of Success

Entrepreneurship isn't a one-size-fits-all formula—it's a messy, demanding, and evolving journey. There's no manual or mantra. Success depends on your **vision**, **resilience**, and **ability to iterate constantly**.

You must be ready to **sacrifice comfort**, invest **time, energy, and mental strength**, and push through long, uncertain periods with **patience and grit**. Like bamboo, startups may grow unseen for years—until they finally burst into the light.

🔑 Key Principles to Guide You

1. **Live in the Future**: Don't build for today. Build for where the market will be when your product is ready.

2. **Spot the Gaps**: Look for problems or inefficiencies—every opportunity lies in a problem waiting to be solved.

3. **Write It Down**: Capture observations, insights, and feedback constantly—most don't, and it sets you apart.

4. **Prototype Quickly**: Your MVP is proof of possibility. It validates vision and lets others experience your idea.

5. **Show, Don't Hide**: Share your prototype. Don't fear idea theft—execution matters more than the idea itself.

6. **Iterate Fast**: Make quick, low-effort improvements based on real feedback.

7. **Find a Co-founder**: A complementary partner is vital—no one builds alone.

8. **Mind the Money**: Design a functional business model or secure aligned investors—don't chase valuation hype.

9. **Launch Smart**: Go big on *impact*, not necessarily spending. Be aggressive with marketing within your bandwidth.

10. **Engage Relentlessly**: Follow up with customers. Their evolving needs determine your product's relevance.

11. **Prioritize Sustainable Growth**: Steady growth beats explosive scaling without experience.

12. **Take Calculated Risks**: Know what's at stake. Always have a fallback plan.

🚀 Execution Roadmap: Step-by-Step Building Blocks

Research & Discovery

- Research deeply before building—know the landscape, your competition, and your audience.

- Begin with problems you understand or are personally affected by.

Prototyping & Validation

- Build your **Minimum Viable Product (MVP)**.
- Show it to real users and collect feedback immediately.
- Ask: Is it solving a painful, urgent problem? Is anyone willing to pay?

Skills & Learning

- Hone key skills: communication, sales, marketing, leadership.
- Educate yourself through books, articles, videos, and forums.
- Follow successful entrepreneurs and analyze their journeys.

Habits & Productivity

- Cultivate habits aligned with your long-term goals.
- Eliminate distractions, develop discipline, and optimize your daily routine.

Team Building

- Build an *excellent*, not just good, team.
- Use your social capital: friends, alumni, ex-colleagues.
- If you can't pay, offer long-term vision, ownership, and personal growth.

Legal & Structure

- Register only when confident in your team and idea.
- Set up the right legal entity. Secure patents, trademarks, and agreements.

Product-Market Fit: Your Startup's Lifeline

Product-Market Fit (PMF) means being in a good market with a product that satisfies that market. It's the *most important step*—and often the most overlooked.

- Validate early and often.
- Never assume PMF is "done." Your customer, market, and context will evolve.
- Align your solution precisely with your audience's **urgent needs**.
- Listen. Adjust. Repeat.

Without PMF, all efforts risk being wasted.

Surviving the First Year

You need:

1. **Runway** to survive for 6–12 months.
2. An MVP that **solves one major pain point**.
3. Constant **customer interaction and feedback**.
4. Frugal operations with **bare minimum costs**.
5. A focus on **micro-goals**: First 10 → 40 → 100 customers.

Building a Team Without Paying Them

- Your network is your best asset.
- Show potential in the mission and future upside.
- Lead with **integrity**, **hustle**, and **clarity of purpose**.

Roles of an Entrepreneur

You'll wear many hats:

- Visionary
- Product Developer
- Janitor (yes!)
- Evangelist
- Marketer
- Researcher
- Content Creator
- Team Builder
- Cheerleader

You **cannot outsource your core**—master your business's fundamentals.

☑ Beyond Year One: Scaling Wisely

- **Scalability**: Can your solution handle 10x or 100x users without breaking?
- **Market Size**: Is it large and growing?
- **Timing**: Why now? Is there a shift in tech, user behavior, or access?
- **Team Strength**: Can your team stay the course?

◎ What Truly Matters

- **Revenue > Funding**: Monetization is proof of value.
- **Customers > Conferences**: Stay close to real users, not industry hype.

- **Core Competency**: Own the core skill of your startup—don't outsource it.
- **Reading, Content, and Visibility**: Build authority in your niche.

⚠ What's Overrated & Underrated

Overrated:

- Fundraising and valuations
- Events and startup networking
- Fancy offices and co-working hubs

Underrated:

- Deep customer observation
- Mentorship and community
- Creating domain-specific content
- Reading for skill and clarity
- Forming smart collaborations

🔍 The Subtle Art of Product-Market Fit

Failing to get PMF right causes most startup deaths.

- Many build for themselves, not their market.
- Validate early. Iterate often. Be obsessed with **customer behavior**, not your assumptions.
- You don't need a revolutionary idea—just a new perspective and elegant execution.

✺ Final Thoughts

Startups demand everything. You must lead, follow, execute, sell, market, learn, and teach—all while navigating ambiguity.

Your perspective, humility, and hustle define your trajectory more than any investor, pitch deck, or certificate ever will.

Be the one who observes. Builds. Listens. Adjusts. Persists.

That's the real blueprint to entrepreneurial success.

Epilogue: From the Page to the Path

I've poured into these pages the distilled essence of my experience—my learnings, mistakes, insights, and the tools that shaped my professional & entrepreneurial journey. This book was never meant to be just theory. It's meant to be your companion, your quiet advisor, as you navigate the unpredictable, exhilarating path of building your own business.

You'll find step-by-step guidance throughout. Tools. Frameworks. Perspectives. They're here for you to use, adapt, or challenge. But remember—*they're only tools*. What gives them meaning is how *you* wield them.

Let me put it this way.

You didn't read a book on love before you first felt it. And yet, perhaps later, a page or paragraph about love helped you make sense of it—comforted you, clarified something, gave you words for what you already knew deep inside.

It's the same with starting a business.

You don't *need* this book—or any book—to begin. The desire, the drive, the restlessness inside you—that's already enough. Books like this one might help you find language, focus, or direction. But no amount of reading can replace the experience of *doing*.

You will stumble. You will doubt. You will learn.

And that's exactly how it's meant to be.

So, take what's useful. Leave what's not. Come back to these pages when you need them. But above all—**go build**. The real story of your startup doesn't live in this book. It lives in what you create next.

Additional Resources

🌐 Books

1. **The Lean Startup** – *Eric Ries*

    A must-read on building businesses through validated learning, rapid experimentation,

    and iteration.

2. **Zero to One** – *Peter Thiel with Blake Masters*

    Offers insights into innovation, monopolies, and building unique businesses.

3. **Start with Why** – *Simon Sinek*

    Focuses on purpose-driven leadership and how to inspire customers and teams.

4. **The $100 Startup** – *Chris Guillebeau*

    A practical guide for launching a business with low capital.

5. **Rework** – *Jason Fried & David Heinemeier Hansson*

    Challenges conventional startup wisdom with a minimalist approach to building

    businesses.

6. **Good to Great** – *Jim Collins*

Explores how good companies transition to greatness and the factors behind long-term

success.

7. **The E-Myth Revisited** – *Michael E. Gerber*

   Breaks down why most small businesses fail and how to build systems that scale.

8. **The Hard Thing About Hard Things** – *Ben Horowitz*

   Raw and practical insights from one of Silicon Valley's most respected entrepreneurs.

9. **Business Model Generation** – *Alexander Osterwalder & Yves Pigneur*

   A visual and strategic handbook for designing, analyzing, and improving business models.

10. **Hooked: How to Build Habit-Forming Products** – *Nir Eyal*

    A psychological framework for building products people keep coming back to.

🌐 Web Resources

- **Y Combinator Startup Library** – https://www.ycombinator.com/library

  Practical essays and talks from founders and mentors at the world's top startup

  accelerator.

- **First Round Review** – https://review.firstround.com

  Deep-dive startup lessons from operators at top companies.

- **Paul Graham's Essays** – http://www.paulgraham.com

    Insightful essays from the co-founder of Y Combinator.

- **SaaStr Blog** – https://www.saastr.com/blog/

    Great for SaaS founders—tips on scaling, fundraising, and growth.

- **Harvard Business Review (HBR)** – https://hbr.org

    Strategic and leadership insights for entrepreneurs and executives.

🎬 Videos & Podcasts

- **How I Built This** (Podcast by Guy Raz – NPR)

    Stories behind the people who built iconic businesses.

- **Masters of Scale** (Podcast by Reid Hoffman)

    Lessons on scaling from founders of Airbnb, LinkedIn, and more.

- **Stanford eCorner** (Talks by Stanford faculty & guests)

    Entrepreneurial leadership, ethics, and innovation lessons.

Bonus Chapters

APPENDIX-1
30-Day Business Launch Checklist

Here's a comprehensive 30-day Business Launch Checklist designed to help entrepreneurs expedite the launch of their new ventures. While it's presented here as a daily schedule, you can also adapt it into a weekly format—completing 6–7 (or more) tasks based on your availability and level of engagement. This checklist covers key steps from ideation to launch:

Week 1: Ideation and Planning

1. **Define Your Business Idea**

    o   Identify your product/service and value proposition.

2. **Conduct Market Research**

    o   Analyze industry trends, target market, and competitors.

3. **Develop a Business Plan**

    o   Write an outline including your business model, objectives, strategies, and financial projections.

4. **Choose a Business Name & Get it Registered**

    o   Select a memorable name and ensure it aligns with your brand.

- Check availability and register with relevant authorities

5. **Finalize a Location for your Business**
   - Decide a location considering relevant factors for your business.

6. **Determine Your Legal Structure**
   - Decide between LLC, sole proprietorship, corporation, etc.

7. **Obtain Necessary Permits/Licenses**
   - Research and apply for required permits and licenses.

Week 2: Financial Setup

8. **Set Up a Business Bank Account**
   - Open an account separate from personal finances.

9. **Create a Budget**
   - Outline your startup costs and ongoing expenses.

10. **Establish an Accounting System**
    - Choose accounting software or hire an accountant.

11. **Explore Funding Options**
    - Research grants, loans, or investors if needed.

12. **Build a Financial Model**
    - Create projections for revenue, expenses, and profitability.

13. **Set Up Payment Processing**

- Decide on methods for accepting payments (credit cards, PayPal, etc.).

14. **Find a Bookkeeper**
    - Consider hiring or consulting with a professional for financial management.

Week 3: Branding and Marketing

15. **Develop a Brand Identity**
    - Design a logo and choose brand colors and fonts.

16. **Create a Website**
    - Register a domain and build a professional website with necessary functionalities.

17. **Set Up Social Media Profiles**
    - Create accounts on relevant platforms (Facebook, Instagram, LinkedIn).

18. **Establish Your Unique Selling Proposition (USP)**
    - Clearly define what sets you apart from competitors.

19. **Craft Marketing Strategy**
    - Consider digital marketing, content, and social media strategies.

20. **Plan for Launch Promotions**
    - Develop ideas for discounts, giveaways, or pre-launch events.

21. **Create Marketing Materials**

- Prepare business cards, brochures, and online content.

Week 4: Launch Preparation

22. **Finalize Your Website**
    - Ensure your site is optimized for SEO and mobile responsiveness.

23. **Social Media Scheduling**
    - Schedule posts and content leading up to the launch.

24. **Engage with Early Customers**
    - Reach out for feedback or beta testing opportunities.

25. **Develop a FAQ Section**
    - Anticipate questions from customers and prepare answers.

26. **Train Your Team**
    - If applicable, ensure your staff is trained and ready to assist customers.

27. **Perform a Soft Launch**
    - Test your product/service with a small audience for feedback.

28. **Refine Based on Feedback**
    - Make necessary adjustments based on initial customer reactions.

Launch Day and Beyond

29. **Launch Your Business**

    o Officially open your business and execute your marketing plan.

30. **Monitor and Adjust**

    o Track performance metrics, gather customer feedback, and be ready to adapt strategies as needed.

Tips for Success

- **Stay Flexible**: Be prepared to pivot based on feedback and market conditions.

- **Network**: Connect with other entrepreneurs and potential customers early on.

- **Seek Help**: Don't hesitate to ask for advice or assistance from mentors and experts.

This checklist can be customized to suit your specific business needs and industry.

APPENDIX-2
Business Budgeting Checklist

Here's a **Business Budgeting Checklist** designed especially **for entrepreneurs and small business owners**. You can use this **monthly, quarterly, or annually** to stay on top of your finances and plan like a pro.

☑ **Business Budgeting Checklist**

🔍 **1. Review Income & Revenue**

- **Analyze past revenue data (last month/quarter/year)**
- **Forecast income based on sales trends or contracts**
- **Account for seasonal fluctuations or market shifts**
- **Identify all sources of income (product sales, services, partnerships, investments)**

💰 **2. List Fixed Costs (Same Every Month)**

- **Rent or mortgage**
- **Salaries (non-commission)**
- **Internet and utilities**
- **Software subscriptions**
- **Insurance premiums**
- **Loan repayments**

☑ 3. Estimate Variable Costs (Fluctuate Monthly)

- Inventory or raw materials
- Marketing & advertising
- Shipping & packaging
- Travel or business meals
- Hourly wages or contractor payments
- Commissions or bonuses
- Utilities with variable rates

🛠 4. Factor in One-Time or Irregular Expenses

- Equipment purchases or upgrades
- Business events or conferences
- Website redesigns or tech upgrades
- Legal or consulting fees
- Seasonal inventory investments

🔒 5. Plan for Emergencies & Savings

- Allocate funds for a cash reserve or emergency fund
- Set aside savings for future business growth (e.g., expansion, new hires)
- Budget for taxes (federal, state, local, VAT/GST)

📊 6. Monitor & Adjust Regularly

- Compare actual vs. projected income
- Compare actual vs. projected expenses

- Track cash flow monthly
- Identify overspending categories
- Adjust budget based on new data or priorities

7. Set & Revisit Financial Goals

- Set monthly/quarterly financial goals (revenue, savings, debt reduction)
- Monitor goal progress
- Adjust your strategy if goals aren't being met
- Celebrate wins (even small ones)!

Bonus Tips:

- Use accounting software (QuickBooks, Xero, Wave) to automate tracking
- Review your budget at the same time each month
- Keep receipts and digital copies of all transactions
- Always budget with some wiggle room for unexpected expenses

APPENDIX-3
Business Compliance Checklist

TL;DR – Your Business Compliance Checklist

☑ Apply for your **EIN** (IRS)

☑ Check for **State & Local Tax IDs**

☑ Identify & apply for **licenses and permits** (federal/state/local)

☑ Research your **tax obligations** (sales, excise, etc.)

☑ Consult a pro or tax software to stay compliant

Get the **right insurance** based on your business model

☑ Check for **other kinds of trade permit/ factory licenses etc., as applicable to your location**

☑ Sleep better at night knowing you're covered

APPENDIX-4
Business Registration Essentials Checklist

(Global Edition)

Step	Why It Matters
Choose your business structure	Sets the legal tone for taxes and liability
Reserve and register your business name	Secures your brand identity
Get national and local tax IDs	Required for taxes, hiring, and banking
Register with national authorities	Makes your business legally operational
Apply for business licenses/permits	Ensures you're operating legally in your industry
Get VAT or GST numbers if needed	For sales and international compliance

Step	Why It Matters
Open a business bank account	Keeps finances organized and separate
Stay compliant	Keep up with taxes, renewals, and reporting obligations

APPENDIX-5
Checklist for Choosing a Name for Your Business

■ **Business Name Checklist**

1. Understand What a Good Name Needs to Do

- Is the name **memorable**, easy to pronounce and recall?
- Is it **relevant** to your product, service, values, or audience?
- Is it **unique** and not easily confused with competitors?
- Is it **flexible** enough to grow with your business?
- Is it **digitally available** (domain name and social handles)?
- Can it be **trademarked** and legally protected?

2. Define Your Brand Identity

- Clarified your **mission** and **vision**
- Identified your **target audience**
- Considered your **industry** and **niche**
- Chosen a **brand tone** (e.g., fun, classy, bold, professional)
- Ensured the name reflects your brand's **core essence**

3. Brainstorm Ideas

- Used **word association** techniques
- Created a **mind map** with central themes
- Tried **mash-up** names (e.g., Netflix = Internet + Flicks)
- Explored meaningful words from **foreign languages**
- Experimented with **acronyms**
- Played with **puns or clever wordplay**
- Generated a **long list** of at least 20–30 name ideas without judging them

4. Narrow Down the List

- Shortlisted 3–5 top contenders
- Checked each for:
    - Easy spelling and pronunciation
    - Clear relevance to your brand
    - Positive emotional or visual association
    - No negative or inappropriate meanings (especially in other languages)
- Verified **domain name availability**
- Searched for **existing trademarks** (e.g., via USPTO.gov)
- Checked **social media handle availability**

5. Test Your Top Choices

- Collected feedback from:
    - Target audience
    - Friends, mentors, and peers

- Asked:
    - "What does this name make you think of?"
    - "How would you spell it?"
    - "What type of business would you assume this is?"
- Made adjustments based on helpful feedback

6. Make It Official

- **Purchased the domain name**
- **Reserved social media handles** (consistently across major platforms)
- **Registered your business name** locally or nationally
- **Filed for trademark protection** if necessary

💡 Final Tip

- Does the name **feel right** and align with your long-term vision?
- Are you **excited to build a brand** around this name?

APPENDIX-6
SAMPLE TEMPLATE FOR FUNDING

📊 Startup Pitch Deck Template for Funding

❀ 1. Cover Slide

- **Company Name**
- Logo / Tagline
- Your Name & Title
- Contact Information
- Date

Example:

LunaRise Skincare

"Plant-powered skincare that heals from within"

Jane Doe, Founder & CEO | <u>janedoe@email.com</u> | <u>www.lunariseskin.com</u>

🚀 2. Problem

Clearly describe the problem you're solving. Make it relatable and urgent.

- What pain points do customers face?
- Who experiences this problem?

- Why hasn't this been solved effectively?

Tip: Use a stat, story, or quote to make it emotional.

💡 3. Solution

Introduce your product or service as the solution.

- What have you built?
- How does it solve the problem better than existing options?
- What is the unique value proposition?

Optional: Include screenshots, product demo visuals, or a short explainer video link.

🏆 4. Market Opportunity

Show the size of the market and your potential for scale.

- Total Addressable Market (TAM)
- Serviceable Available Market (SAM)
- Serviceable Obtainable Market (SOM)
- Target customer profile

Use real numbers + charts to paint a big-picture opportunity.

💸 5. Business Model

Explain how you make money.

- Pricing strategy
- Revenue streams
- Unit economics (if applicable)

- Lifetime Value (LTV) vs Customer Acquisition Cost (CAC)

☑ 6. Traction / Milestones

Show your progress to date and why now is the time to invest.

- Key achievements (sales, users, partnerships, media)
- Growth metrics (monthly revenue, user base, retention)
- Customer testimonials or case studies

Tip: Use visuals or timelines for clarity.

ⓥⓢ 7. Competitive Landscape

Explain how you're different and better than alternatives.

- Who are your key competitors?
- What makes your approach unique? (USP)
- Competitive matrix (you vs others)

⚒ 8. Product Roadmap

Show what's next for your business.

- Short-term milestones (next 6–12 months)
- Long-term vision (3–5 years)
- Planned features, markets, or products

👥 9. Team

Highlight the people behind the business.

- Founders and key team members
- Backgrounds & relevant experience

- Advisors (if any)

Tip: Investors often back teams more than ideas—show them why you're the right people.

💰 10. Financials

Share a high-level view of your financial projections.

- Revenue & expense forecast (3–5 years)
- Burn rate and runway
- Break-even point (if applicable)

Include a simple chart showing revenue growth and costs.

📦 11. Funding Ask

Tell investors exactly what you're looking for.

- How much are you raising?
- How will you use the funds? (team, product, marketing, etc.)
- What's the expected runway or milestones with this funding?

Example:

"We're raising **$500,000** to support product development, customer acquisition, and hiring key team members. This will give us a **12-month runway** and help us grow from 10K users to 100K."

🖼 12. Closing Slide / Thank You

End with a strong, memorable note.

- Recap your vision or mission

- Add contact info again
- Call-to-action: "Let's talk," "Join us," or "Be part of the journey"

📇 Optional Add-on Slides

- **Customer Testimonials or Use Cases**
- **Social Proof (press, awards, partnerships)**
- **Exit Strategy / M&A Potential**
- **Risk Factors and Mitigation**

🛠 Format Options:

- **PowerPoint / Keynote / Google Slides**
- Keep text **brief and visual**
- Use **infographics, charts, and icons** to break up text
- Keep the deck to **12–15 slides** max

Glossary

1. Angel Investor
An individual who provides capital for a startup, usually in exchange for equity or convertible debt. Often the first outside investor.

2. Bootstrapping
Starting and growing a business using personal finances or operating revenue—no external funding involved.

3. Burn Rate
The rate at which a startup spends money before generating positive cash flow. High burn rate = risky runway.

4. Business Model
A company's plan for making a profit, detailing how it creates, delivers, and captures value.

5. Cap Table (Capitalization Table)
A spreadsheet or table that shows the equity ownership breakdown of a company, including shares, options, and investor stakes.

6. Churn Rate
The percentage of customers who stop using your product/service within a given time frame. High churn = red flag.

7. Customer Acquisition Cost (CAC)
The total cost of acquiring a new customer, including marketing, sales, and operational expenses.

8. Disruptive Innovation
An innovation that creates a new market by significantly altering or replacing an existing one.

9. Elevator Pitch
A concise, compelling summary of your business idea, designed to be delivered in 30-60 seconds.

10. Equity
Ownership in a company, typically expressed as shares or a percentage of the total business.

11. Exit Strategy
A plan for how the founder(s) and investors will eventually cash out or sell their stake in the company.

12. Freemium
A pricing strategy where the basic version of a product is free, but advanced features must be paid for.

13. Funding Rounds (Seed, Series A, B, C...)
Stages of investment that a startup goes through to raise capital, typically growing in size and investor sophistication with each round.

14. Incubator
A program or organization that helps startups grow by offering resources like office space, mentorship, and seed funding.

15. IPO (Initial Public Offering)
The process of offering shares of a private company to the public for the first time.

16. Lean Startup
A methodology that emphasizes building MVPs, testing assumptions quickly, and iterating based on customer feedback.

17. Market Fit (Product-Market Fit)
The degree to which a product satisfies a strong market demand—crucial for startup success.

18. Minimum Viable Product (MVP)
A basic version of a product that allows you to collect maximum customer feedback with minimum effort.

19. Pivot
A fundamental change in business strategy based on feedback, failure, or new opportunity.

20. Runway
The amount of time your startup can survive before running out of money, based on your burn rate.

21. SaaS (Software as a Service)
A business model that delivers software over the internet on a subscription basis.

22. Scalability
A business's ability to grow revenue exponentially with minimal increases in cost.

23. Seed Capital
The initial funding used to start a business, often from founders, family, friends, or angel investors.

24. Stakeholder
Any person or group affected by or invested in a business—includes employees, customers, investors, and suppliers.

25. Term Sheet
A non-binding agreement that outlines the basic terms and conditions under which an investment will be made.

26. Unicorn
A privately held startup valued at over $1 billion.

27. Valuation
The estimated worth of a company, often based on financial projections, assets, and market size.

28. Venture Capital (VC)
Financing provided to startups with high growth potential in exchange for equity.

29. Vertical Market
A market that targets a specific industry or niche, such as healthcare, fintech, or edtech.

30. Wear Many Hats
A phrase referring to startup founders/employees who take on multiple roles due to lean team structures.

31. Balance Sheet
A financial statement showing a company's assets, liabilities, and equity at a specific point in time.

32. Budget
A financial plan that estimates revenue and expenses over a period—used to manage and control cash flow.

33. Break-even Point
The point at which total revenue equals total costs—no profit, no loss. Every entrepreneur's initial victory lap.

34. Cash Flow
The movement of money in and out of a business. Positive cash flow = healthy; negative = danger zone.

35. Cost of Goods Sold (COGS)
The direct costs of producing the products sold by a business—materials, labor, etc.

36. Depreciation
The gradual decrease in the value of a physical asset over time due to wear and tear or obsolescence.

37. EBITDA (Earnings Before Interest, Taxes, Depreciation, and Amortization)
A measure of a company's profitability often used to compare financial performance.

38. Forecasting
Predicting future revenue, expenses, or market trends using historical data, market research, and a dash of entrepreneurial optimism.

39. Gross Margin
The difference between revenue and COGS, expressed as a percentage. It shows how efficiently a company produces goods.

40. Income Statement (Profit & Loss Statement)
A report showing a company's revenues, expenses, and profit (or loss) over a specific time period.

41. Liabilities
What a company owes—loans, accounts payable, mortgages, etc.

42. Net Profit (or Net Income)
What remains from revenue after all expenses have been deducted. Also known as "the reason we're doing this."

43. Operating Expenses (OPEX)
The day-to-day costs of running a business, such as rent, utilities, salaries, and marketing.

44. ROI (Return on Investment)
A performance measure used to evaluate the efficiency of an investment.

45. Working Capital
The difference between current assets and current liabilities. It measures liquidity and short-term financial health.

46. Business Plan
A document outlining a company's goals, strategies, target market, and financial projections—used to guide operations and attract investors.

47. Competitive Advantage
What makes your business stand out from the competition—could be price, quality, innovation, or customer service.

48. Customer Lifetime Value (CLTV)
A prediction of how much revenue a customer will bring during their entire relationship with your business.

49. KPI (Key Performance Indicator)
A measurable value that indicates how effectively a company is achieving its key business objectives.

50. Limited Liability
A legal structure that protects owners from being personally liable for company debts (e.g., in a Pvt Ltd or LLC).

51. Market Segmentation
Dividing a market into distinct groups based on demographics, behavior, or needs to target them effectively.

52. Mission Statement
A brief statement that defines a company's core purpose and values.

53. Onboarding
The process of welcoming and training new employees—or customers—to get them up and running.

54. SOP (Standard Operating Procedure)
A documented step-by-step guide for routine business activities to ensure consistency and efficiency.

55. Target Market
The specific group of people your product or service is intended for.

56. Value Proposition
A clear explanation of how your product solves customers' problems or improves their situation—why they should choose you.

57. A/B Testing
An experiment where two versions (A and B) of a marketing asset (email, webpage, ad) are compared to see which performs better.

58. B2B (Business-to-Business)
A business model where products or services are sold from one business to another.

59. B2C (Business-to-Consumer)
A business model where products or services are sold directly to consumers.

60. Brand Awareness
The extent to which consumers recognize and are familiar with your brand—essential for visibility and growth.

61. Buyer Persona
A fictional, detailed profile of your ideal customer based on research, used to guide marketing strategies.

62. Call to Action (CTA)
A phrase or button encouraging users to take a specific action—like "Buy Now," "Sign Up," or "Get Started."

63. Click-Through Rate (CTR)
The percentage of people who clicked on a link or ad compared to how many saw it—used to measure engagement.

64. Conversion Rate
The percentage of users who take a desired action (buy, sign up, download) after interacting with your marketing.

65. Content Marketing
Creating and sharing valuable content (blogs, videos, etc.) to attract, engage, and convert customers.

66. Customer Journey
The complete experience a customer has with your brand—from awareness to purchase to loyalty.

67. Digital Marketing
Marketing efforts using digital channels like search engines, social media, email, and websites.

68. Funnel (Marketing Funnel or Sales Funnel)
The step-by-step process of turning leads into customers—typically includes Awareness, Interest, Decision, and Action.

69. Growth Hacking
Using creative, low-cost strategies to acquire and retain customers—often involving unconventional marketing tactics.

70. Influencer Marketing
Partnering with social media influencers or content creators to promote your product or brand.

71. Lead Generation
The process of attracting and converting strangers into prospects or customers.

72. Lifetime Value (LTV)
A forecast of the total revenue a customer will generate over their relationship with your brand.

73. Market Penetration
A strategy to increase market share by selling more of your existing products to your current market.

74. Niche Market
A small, specialized segment of a broader market with specific needs and preferences.

75. Omnichannel Marketing
Providing a seamless customer experience across multiple platforms—online, offline, mobile, and social.

76. Retargeting (or Remarketing)
Online ads targeted at users who previously visited your website or interacted with your brand.

77. USP (Unique Selling Proposition)
The factor that makes your brand or product different—and better—than the competition.

About the Author

William O. Ivan is a seasoned educator, mentor, and business coach with a deep-rooted passion for entrepreneurship. With extensive experience in leadership roles across major manufacturing organizations and a successful track record of teaching entrepreneurship at some of the country's top business schools, William brings both practical know-how and academic depth to his work. Many of his students have gone on to become serial entrepreneurs—a testament to his impact and guidance.

Entrepreneurship isn't just something William teaches—it's a way of life he fully embodies. He has spent decades immersed in the business world, embracing the highs and lows, the long nights and breakthrough moments. His insights come not just from observation, but from being deeply engaged in the entrepreneurial journey himself.

Through his years of experience, William has come to understand that entrepreneurship is as much about mindset as it is about methodology. It demands resilience, adaptability, strategic thinking, and the courage to take bold yet calculated risks. It's about building a vision, rallying people around it, and persisting when the odds seem insurmountable.

This book is his way of giving back—of sharing the lessons, truths, and tools he has accumulated over the years. With a blend of practical advice, real-world insights, and stories of both failure and success, William aims to equip aspiring entrepreneurs with the confidence and clarity to forge their own paths.

www.ingramcontent.com/pod-product-compliance
Lightning Source LLC
LaVergne TN
LVHW010216070526
838199LV00062B/4614